THE A-Z OF
INTERNATIONAL SCHOOL LEADERSHIP

SIMON WATSON

SERIES EDITOR: ROY BLATCHFORD

JOHN CATT
FROM HODDER EDUCATION

Although every effort has been made to ensure that website addresses are correct at time of going to press, Hodder Education cannot be held responsible for the content of any website mentioned in this book. It is sometimes possible to find a relocated web page by typing in the address of the home page for a website in the URL window of your browser.

Hachette UK's policy is to use papers that are natural, renewable and recyclable products and made from wood grown in well-managed forests and other controlled sources. The logging and manufacturing processes are expected to conform to the environmental regulations of the country of origin.

To order, please visit www.johncatt.com or contact Customer Service at education@hachette.co.uk / +44 (0)1235 827827.

ISBN: 978 1 0360 0505 4

First published in 2024 by
John Catt from Hodder Education,
An Hachette UK Company
15 Riduna Park, Station Road,
Melton, Woodbridge IP12 1QT
www.johncatt.com

Typeset in the UK.

Printed in the UK.

A catalogue record for this title is available from the British Library.

MIX
Paper | Supporting responsible forestry
FSC
www.fsc.org
FSC™ C104740

DEDICATION

To Lucy, Ana, Miranne, Kat and Pi

for their love as we traverse the world

ACKNOWLEDGEMENTS

Sincere thanks to Roy Blatchford whose insight, enthusiasm and restless pursuit of excellence has improved the lives of countless children and educators over many years. I am grateful for his suggestions, which have contributed to and improved this book, but of course any errors remain mine.

Thanks go to all my wonderful colleagues at St Christopher's School, Bahrain, whose professionalism and dedication have supported my leadership over the past six years. Similar thanks, too, to the staff at Kolej Tuanku Jaafar, Malaysia, where I learned much and enjoyed the challenges of a school in 'the jungle'.

To Peter Wellby who appointed me to my first senior leadership position at Copenhagen International School, without his support I would not have been able to write this book.

And to John Paige, who provides a guiding perspective on life.

CONTENTS

Section Two

FOREWORD

One of the paradoxes at the heart of many international schools – and no two are alike – is that they are simultaneously inward and outward facing. An international school – say in Switzerland, Qatar or Bangkok – has students from all parts of the globe who commute in and out of the school every term.

At the same time, once on campus, and taught often by ex-pats living in their community bubbles, the students form a tightly knit body which focuses quite properly on its own mutual wellbeing. And boarding houses accentuate that dimension.

Leaders in these high-performing international schools recognise the importance of their students looking outwards. Given their multi-lingual, multi-cultural make-up, this is not difficult. Their families live in different time zones; their social media connections, work experience placements and school journeys are richly global.

Students aged 3–18 in these settings reflect deeply on the following key questions, as part of their studies and as part of everyday life on campus:

1. Do I know and learn about what is happening in the world?
2. Do I value other people's culture and differences, as well as seeing their similarities to my own?
3. Am I able to converse in other languages, having enough of an understanding to appreciate that the world looks different through different linguistic constructs?
4. Am I digitally confident, having the cultural skills to collaborate, negotiate and weigh up action critically?
5. Do I have the confidence to take action, to reach out to others, to travel, to take personal and collective responsibility for sustainability in the world?

Addressing those questions within their internationally focused curriculum helps students – and staff – embed an appreciation of different cultures, religions and attitudes which often collide and confuse. That ability to see oneself through another culture and language is fundamentally enriching.

****

Simon Watson's extensive experience as a leader of schools across the globe is evident throughout the book. His values and acute cultural awareness, combined with a strong sense of 'walking the talk' in corridors and classrooms, provide a guidebook of distinction.

One hallmark of many international schools is the inevitable churn of students, teachers and leaders. Here he writes perceptively about headteachers moving into new positions:

> The initial year for a head will be one of clarity, when a new head can see the issues and celebrate the exceptional. This is a time for honest reflection and setting the agenda for the next few years. The moments of clarity will diminish as the landscape becomes familiar and loses its immediacy. The head is soon institutionalised and has to take greater and greater responsibility for the school, so that the problems that existed when the head arrived cease to be the previous head's issues, but firmly become the new head's problems and responsibility.

In my enjoyable and instructive experiences of inspecting and reviewing international schools, I see leaders and staff alike thriving on the wonderful opportunity to explore the world and be challenged by the truly unexpected.

In common with all books in the series, Section One is ordered under the A–Z alphabetical headings. Section Two presents further material for professional development.

From **Accountability** and **Belonging**, through **Jabberwockery** and **Monkeys**, to **Xenagogue** and **Zeitgeist**, the text is fun, authoritative and highly readable.

Roy Blatchford, series editor

INTRODUCTION

There are numerous disagreements about the definition of international schools. One such definition is provided by ISC Research, where it defines an international school as a school that:

> delivers a curriculum to any combination of pre-school, primary or secondary students, wholly or partly in English outside an English-speaking country; or,
>
> if a school is in a country where English is one of the official languages, it offers an English-medium curriculum other than the country's national curriculum and the school is international in its orientation.

Like many national schools that exist, there are similarities and differences between international schools, so it makes no sense to talk about 'international schools' as a single entity but to recognise the magnificent diversity of places of learning around the world. This is why there are so many discussions and much variance when it comes to the definition of an international school.

The intention of this A–Z is not to present an academic authority on international school leadership but to provide various windows into the experiences and thoughts of an international school leader. The information may be useful to some, obvious to others; it represents a small aspect of international school leadership that I have enjoyed and been challenged by during my journey to date. Inevitably, there is much overlap between leadership in national education systems, and international school leadership, resulting in areas of this book that are applicable to both.

Just as the typical demographic of the student population has changed over the past 40 years, from a majority of expatriate families to a majority of local families, so, too, has the international schools' scene. There are far more for-profit schools run as businesses than ever before, many emanating from the UK. It does raise the question as to whether some international schooling is a modern day form of colonialism. Is there a difference between a not-for-profit school that has grown organically and evolved over a long period of time in the host country, compared with a for-profit school that is launched with great fanfare, slick marketing and channels money back to a central organisation?

The structure of the book allows each chapter to be read in isolation – there is no need to start at the beginning – but enjoy the freedom of dipping in and out of each part, depending on mood and desire.

As in all schools, the main job of the international school head is to improve student learning. This is done within a complex environment that is composed of many cultures, historical precedents and competing expectations. It is a wonderful life, where days fleetingly pass at a sprint that competes with Usain Bolt.

Parts of the sections on curriculum, expectations, quality, vision and wellbeing, and parts of Section Two, have been utilised from a range of staff (past and present) from St Christopher's School, Bahrain.

> The revolution I'm advocating is based on different principles from those of the standards movement. It is based on a belief in the value of the individual, the right to self-determination, our potential to evolve and live a fulfilled life, and the importance of civic responsibility and respect for others.
>
> Ken Robinson

International school leaders have a unique opportunity to be part of the revolution. Only fear holds us back.

SECTION ONE

ACCOUNTABILITY

Higher standards are hard to maintain. It requires the discipline to constantly talk about and remind everyone WHY the organization exists in the first place. It requires that everyone in the organization be held accountable to HOW you do things—to your values and guiding principles.

Simon Sinek

Accountability comes in a multitude of guises. Accreditations and inspections by external agencies are necessary, but not sufficient, hallmarks of quality education in international schools. While an important external measure of quality, they do not, on their own, guarantee exceptional education for learners. The role of the international school leader is to ensure the standards of accreditation are used to build upon best practice and create new educational boundaries.

Accreditation agencies update their standards framework regularly, keeping schools aligned to the current and best educational practice and supporting schools to continually improve. The benefits of accreditations/inspections are manifold, with improving standards being at their core.

School leaders are mindful of the marketing opportunities that accreditation provides, attracting prospective families and teachers. During interviews the refrains of 'I want to work in an "outstanding school"', a reference to the British Schools Overseas inspection, or 'I want to be at an accredited school', are often cited by candidates as a reason for their application.

The list of agencies below is not intended to be exhaustive but to provide a range of possible options for international school leaders.

Accreditations are designed to be developmental, whereas inspections are judgements on practice at a point in time. It should be noted that the inspection judgements or accreditation development points made are only as good as the team visiting the school, and the willingness of the school to act on the recommendations.

While the various accreditation/inspection agencies will tell you that they all have rigorous protocols and training in place, there is clearly an eclectic mix of observations being made during their visits, with disparate teams requesting different data when measuring schools against the same standards.

Some schools may have more than one accreditation/inspection, as this gives them access to a wider network, enhances the marketing opportunities of the school and, of course, provides further external measures for improvement. Some agencies have a history of working together, such as the Council of International Schools (CIS) and the New England Association of Schools and Colleges (NEASC), and will arrange a joint visit, thus reducing the duplication of effort and resources on schools.

Accreditation should not be confused with programme authorisation. For example, the International Baccalaureate Organization (IBO) demands compliance to its standards for each of its particular programmes, but they are very much specific to the IBO's programme. A school that offers at least one of the IB programmes will have regular evaluations to ensure 'that the standards and practices of its IB programme(s) are being maintained'. The IBO will only be interested in its own programmes. If a school offers the IB diploma programme, the IBO will evaluate the school's adherence with its own standards for the IB diploma programme and will not be interested in the rest of what happens in the school. In contrast, an accreditation/inspection visit is generally concerned with the quality of education in the whole school, although phase accreditations/inspections are possible.

ACCREDITATION AGENCIES

There are various accreditation/inspection choices available to school leaders, although how much choice the school actually has will depend upon a multitude of factors. Does the school have an existing kitemark through its affiliation to a particular external evaluation? Will the local market allow a change of accreditation/inspection? Is the identity of the school intimately connected to the accrediting agency? The latter happens with some British schools, for example, that project an identity that references cultural symbols from the UK. Some of these symbols may be, at best, outdated and, at worst, offensive to the local context.

Regardless of the accreditation/inspection agency, a school leader who does not insist on their school having an external validation would require exceptional reasons as to why this was the case.

Council of International Schools (CIS)

This is one of the most well-established agencies that is not aligned with a particular country's educational system. Schools across the world are accredited by CIS and these include schools with an affinity to a particular national system such as a British or American education.

The Council states on its website:

> As a leader in the field of school evaluation and accreditation worldwide, we provide a unique international accreditation with a focus on student learning and global citizenship.

Council of British International Schools (COBIS)

COBIS is a UK-based organisation that introduced its own accreditation in 2017. It is becoming increasingly popular with international schools that have a connection to the UK, whether through name or curriculum. It states that schools that follow its accreditation will:

> Gain valuable insight into your progress benchmarked against the best British and international practice, whilst working on your development priorities.

New England Association of Schools and Colleges (NEASC)

This US-based organisation is used by many overseas international schools that offer a US-style high school diploma. This accreditation provides the required recognition for US colleges that accept high school diplomas from international schools. There are many other US-based organisations providing accreditation that will authorise a school to offer a high school diploma. NEASC states that their accreditation will help:

> to assess, support, and promote high quality education for all students through accreditation, professional assistance, and pursuit of best practices.

British Schools Overseas (BSO)

This organisation is primarily used by British international schools and is an inspection, rather than an accreditation. At the time of writing, there are 215 international schools listed on the Department for Education (DfE) website as having successfully passed a BSO inspection. It should be noted that some schools decide to have phases of their school inspected separately. This may be helpful when there are clearly different strengths across phases or if a school is starting out and only has classes to, say, Year 6.

For a BSO inspection, a team of peers, trained by one of the three organisations that currently have authority from the DfE in the UK, will inspect a school against certain standards based on the UK's national inspection system (Ofsted) and decide whether the school has met these standards.

PROCESSES

With an accreditation, there are very clear structures to put in place that the accreditation agency recommends as best practice. Chairs and co-chairs of various committees are expected to organise and manage discussions and improvements over a defined period of time. All stakeholders must be included in the developmental process, with focus group meetings for parents. Student agency is of high importance, as is a genuine desire to reflect on the school's practice and improve all aspects of a school's operations.

It is very much left to the school leaders to decide how to proceed with an inspection knowing, however, that the inspection team will require some very specific information that they will triangulate in their meetings with governors, parents, students and, of course, teachers.

Practice varies widely across schools and leaders as to how an accreditation or inspection is approached.

Some leaders will have the staff at 'DEFCON 1' for as much as a year before an inspection, creating unnecessary stress and doing little to support staff wellbeing. Others take a more measured approach, ensuring that the day-to-day practice is of high quality and then focusing on the particulars of inspection with around six weeks to go.

An accreditation is designed for continuous improvement of practice and, therefore, needs to be strategically planned, over a period of years, with regular review points that allow for corrections to the plan. But, like inspections, the strategy adopted for accreditations is still very much dependent on the school leader.

The accreditation route provides a strong mechanism for ceaseless evolution, benchmarked against the best international standards. It is inclusive and generative in its approach; collaboration is central to its philosophy – a partnership between the accreditation agency and the full school community. Inspection is done to a school.

School leaders seldom have the choice of a clean slate when it comes to deciding whether to choose accreditation or inspection or both. Other schools in the country or region may dictate a particular approach through their own accreditation/inspection choices. Sometimes the national system plays an important part, as in the UAE: the Dubai Schools Inspection Bureau (DSIB), in collaboration with the Knowledge and Human Development Authority (KHDA), inspects all schools every year.

It would be a brave school leader who does not fall into line with the majority, particularly if their employment hinges on the outcome of an accreditation/inspection.

ASIDE

There are countless research articles demonstrating that a blame-focused approach does not yield improved performance, and nobody wants colleagues who only improve because of a rewards system. A rewards methodology is inherently iniquitous, no matter how much we try to be objective.

- Who should be held accountable?
- Should we hold people accountable only to their contracts, policy and job descriptions or, as Sinek[1] states, to the values, principles and guiding statements?
- Is accountability done to someone or is it a shared process?
- Does accountability require a range of processes depending on the 'why' and the 'how' of the school?
- Should there be a greater emphasis in schools on team accountability rather than individual accountability?
- Is there an optimum balance between 'stick' and 'carrot' or is this an outdated attitude to drive improvement?

---

1   Sinek, S. (2009) *Start with Why: How Great Leaders Inspire Everyone to Take Action.* New York: Penguin Group (USA) Inc.

BELONGING

I've learned that people will forget what you said, people will forget what you did, but people will never forget how you made them feel.

Attributed to Maya Angelou

Creating a sense of belonging for all the community has always been the role of a school leader. The political agenda now has a focus on this in all western organisations. Diversity, equity and inclusion (DEI) is an area that will require courage, sensitivity, direct intervention, clear thinking and regular communication.

There are other acronyms that reference the DEI movement; a popular one is DEIJ (diversity, equity, inclusion and justice). It is necessary for the international school leader to know and stay up to date with this fast-changing political and cultural topography, and ascertain how it fits into their local context. It is highly unlikely that the UK or US discourse on DEI will transport seamlessly to their host country.

It is relatively easy for the international school leader, should they wish, to dismiss new national or global initiatives as being the latest trend or wait too long before doing something about them. Clearly, work on DEI is the essence of what leaders should be promoting in schools, but the adaptive leadership skills required may at first appear too much for some heads to manage.

Maybe the current generation of leaders should make way for Generation Z who seems to have DEI encoded into their DNA. Schools in countries with specific legal constraints will not be able to promote LGBTQ+ rights and this could lead to a lazy or weak head disregarding the whole point of DEI practices and continuing with the status quo.

DEI in international schools requires much work. Many schools use nationality statistics as a marketing tool; the number of different nationalities is used as a proxy for internationalism, for inclusion and diversity. However, if one scratches under the surface, how many international schools expect this diverse group of learners to assimilate the culture of the majority group? Inclusion is not about accepting the prevailing culture of the majority but is about creating a new culture that respects and draws upon the multitude of community life experiences that intersect.

NOT LEADING ON DEI

A leader has to be clear on their own values before they can lead on DEI. This may be the biggest obstacle for DEI practices to change in some schools. If the leader believes that the current public discourse on DEI in all its various tenets is no more than liberal 'wokery', then there is never going to be any worthwhile change; there will never be a culture of belonging.

Or perhaps the leader self-regulates to allow an outward acceptance of DEI but does nothing to actually change attitudes and practices. There would be a disconnect between the values they promote and the absence of virtues.

These may be the biggest issues that a leader must address before embarking on a systemic DEI programme.

When leaders do not lead, the DEI movement polarises communities. When leaders remain ignorant about the inequities that exist within their own schools, when they do not question their own beliefs, when they do not engage in their own learning, but instead prefer to perpetuate the existing culture – this is when a senior leader would have to seriously question their position in the school. How many times does a disagreement about culture generate the rhetorical response: 'we are a British school so they need to do it our way'?

Not all countries support DEI initiatives and even in those that do, strong feelings between groups within a school community are likely to be extant. This may be yet another incentive for the international school leader not to move forward with DEI initiatives, particularly if a school is in a country or part of a country where there is no national discourse on DEI or, even worse, where there is outward antagonism towards it.

LEADING ON DEI

Leading on DEI takes courage and a strong belief in what is morally right. For international school leaders who are accomplished at managing different cultures within the same community, DEI is another aspect of that nuanced approach. DEI is best encapsulated as creating a sense of belonging for all.

A few pointers that may be useful on the DEI journey of an international school leader:

1. Heads should provide the gravitas to 'implement DEI' by initially leading it, together with the appointed DEI person(s).

2. Make sure you are up to date with as much detail as possible around DEI issues; attend courses, read books, discuss with colleagues, follow the public discourse.

3. *Race: The Power of an Illusion*[2] contains critical information about 'race' and how, historically, science was erroneously used to create biological differences between people. The science of today refutes these claims.

4. Agree with your senior leaders that DEI is an integral part of what schools do.

5. Define an achievable DEI strategy that gathers information from all stakeholders. The strategy may consider:

   - adapting DEI approaches to reflect the local culture
   - working with local supporters of DEI who may be better placed to communicate complex and sensitive issues to the wider community

---

2   *Race: The Power of an Illusion* (2023). Documentary series. Available at: https://www.racepowerofanillusion.org/

- engaging staff and students to review the policies and curriculum through a DEI lens
- providing support to those new to the country so that they quickly feel settled and integrated into the community.

6. Ensure that the DEI strategy includes what cannot be addressed because of local laws. Every country has its own challenges when addressing cultural and social issues. Western countries are not immune from difficulties; one has only to look at certain states in the US that have banned books and the teaching of critical race theory.

CELEBRATE DIFFERENCE

There is much to celebrate in international schools. While the three 'Fs' of international schools – flags, food and fayres – are fun, they do not begin to promote the diversity that exists in many international schools. If the three Fs are all that a school does in the name of celebrating differences, then there is a long way to go.

International school leaders are ideally situated to reflect on the complexities and ambiguities of their home country from a distance, and compare their observations to those of the host country in which they live and work. For example, the fundamental British values are: democracy, the rule of law, individual liberty, and mutual respect and tolerance of those with different faiths and beliefs.[3]

But when living in a different country, it raises the question of whether *tolerance* is the right attitude to proselytise towards those with different faiths and beliefs. As Diverse Educators[4] write, 'be where you are celebrated, not tolerated'. And as Amanda Gorman so eloquently writes in her poem *The Hill We Climb*: 'what "just is" isn't always justice'.

---

3   *Promoting fundamental British values as part of SMSC in schools* (2014) Department for Education. Available at: https://assets.publishing.service.gov.uk/media/5a758c9540f0b6397f35f469/SMSC_Guidance_Maintained_Schools.pdf
4   Diverse Educators (2023) Available at: https://www.diverseeducators.co.uk/

All of which is succinctly summarised by Arthur Chan[5]:

Equity is a fact.
Diversity is a choice.
Inclusion is an action.
Belonging is the outcome.

ASIDE

When trying to create a culture of belonging in a school, what metrics provide a measure of progress? Obviously, it will depend on the focus areas that have emerged in the action plan. A few areas for consideration might include:

- the inclusivity of policies in both language and intent
- a review of the curriculum and resources, ensuring provision of diverse representation
- how many student forums there are for honest and supportive communication about inequalities that exist within the school
- a discussion about whether there is authentic student agency
- inclusive learning environments and support for all students
- staff retention recruitment statistics monitored by groups
- staff demographics, using a variety of groupings
- diversity in leadership positions
- staff salary equity.

5   Chan, C. LinkedIn post. Available at: https://www.linkedin.com/feed/update/urn:li:activity:6709122719918755840/

CURRICULUM

Tell me and I forget, teach me and I may remember, involve me and I learn.

Anonymous

According to Dylan Wiliam[6] a curriculum should be:

- Balanced – every child is able to find their passion, and the only way to do that is to ensure that each child has a broad and balanced curriculum.
- Rigorous – powerful ways of thinking are developed through sustained engagement with the discipline.
- Coherent – the totality of experiences mutually reinforce each other.
- Vertically integrated – learning is sequenced so that connections between subjects or topics are clearer.
- Appropriate – avoids creating unattainable expectations on learners so that every learner has a suitable level of challenge.
- Focused – the *most* important aspects are taught, even if this means leaving out other important concepts.
- Relevant – teachers need to connect the curriculum to what their students value.

However, Dylan also comments that these seven principles are in tension and that a curriculum could never deliver all these elements in unison.

---

6   Wiliam, D. (2013) *Redesigning Schooling – 3: Principled curriculum design.* Published by SSAT (© SSAT (The Schools Network) Ltd, 2013). Available at: https://webcontent.ssatuk.co.uk/wp-content/uploads/2020/03/20105155/Redesigning-Schooling-3-Principled-curriculum-design-Dylan-Wiliam.pdf

This is where the astute head needs to understand the context of their school, and the needs of their students and staff. Compromises will be made so the best possible curriculum may be designed; one that engages all learners. In the majority of international schools, the student body will be eager to learn, and there is a significant opportunity for leaders to develop a coherent and comprehensive learning ecosystem.

This should be one of the primary focuses for all educational leaders, but international school leaders may have greater leeway and flexibility than their counterparts in a national system. Much of the time we rightly focus on pedagogy and measure *how well* the curriculum is taught but, where possible, we should also question *what* is taught. Dylan Wiliam notes that 'a bad curriculum taught well is better than a good curriculum taught badly'. This statement has an implicit assumption that the bad curriculum is not 'that bad'. Erroneous understandings, provided they are not too numerous, can be corrected at a later stage, but what about the inherent values we are imparting to students through our curriculum offerings?

Making sure the curriculum is unsurpassed in design will allow teachers to disseminate the requisite knowledge, skills, attitudes and competencies that the global leaders of tomorrow will need to reverse the mess that we have created today.

The Future Ready Curriculum[7] (FRC) is such a framework that guides and engages the school community to advance the mission, vision and values of St Christopher's School, Bahrain.

The purpose of the FRC is to equip students with the contemporary knowledge, skills and understanding necessary to serve as *Role Models for the World*. Through subject-based and experiential learning activities, students will receive distinct opportunities to develop competencies through the following domains.

---

7   St Christopher's School, Bahrain (2023) Available at: https://frc.stchrisapps.com/dashboard/#/homepage

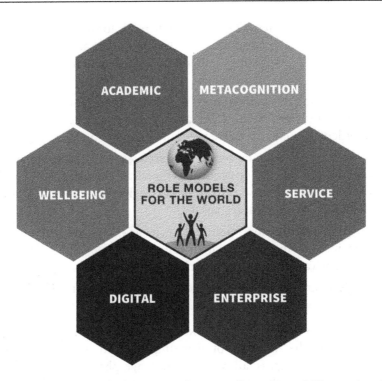

As part of the school's mission, *Education for a Shared Humanity*, this learning journey incorporates student-centred learning activities within the context of the local and global community. Among these are the concept of service, the United Nations Sustainable Development Goals (UNSDGs), internationalism, interculturalism, positive psychology, and social and emotional learning.

Each of the six domains has three competencies. An example of one is shown below.

SER03 — To foster the notion of 'Global Citizenship' through increasing the awareness of rights, responsibilities, and the application of values in order to positively contribute to society while both living & working internationally.

Each competency is then further developed to provide clarification for teachers to use in their planning, as below for SER03.

- To know that the term 'Global Citizen' refers to viewing our identity as one that transcends political and geographical borders, operating as a member of humanity rather than a single nationality. (Develop the notion of internationalism.)
- To develop an appreciation of global governance structures, rights and responsibilities, and the interconnectedness and interdependencies of different countries and populations.
- To recognise and appreciate differences in culture, language, religion, gender, and our common humanity, as well as develop the necessary skills for living in an increasingly diverse world. (Develop the notion of interculturalism.)
- To understand how political and geographical factors can contribute to inequality, which can result in poverty, segregation, and deprivation in different parts of the world.
- To develop the values of fairness, social justice, and inclusion to make the world a more equitable and sustainable place.

The FRC is housed in a bespoke planning platform that stores and organises the schemes of learning, as well as mapping each FRC competency across all subjects and age-phases. This not only demonstrates subject-based learning sequencing and progression, but it also provides all stakeholders with easy access to view learning activities, learning objectives, high-quality resources, assessment methods and FRC competency coverage. There are other planning and mapping platforms available and each head should decide on the most suitable platform for the context of their school. Section Two contains details of all the competencies that have been developed at St Christopher's School, Bahrain.

INTERNATIONAL CURRICULA

The FRC above is just one example of how it is possible to develop a curriculum in the international setting. For some leaders this is an exhilarating prospect; others may have different priorities. There are so many possible resources to start the process.

One place to start is the Organisation for Economic Co-operation and Development (OECD), which carries out much educational research and publishes it free on its website. Other organisations include the United Nations Educational, Scientific and Cultural Organization (UNESCO). In addition, of course, there has been a vast array of educational research on curriculum design.

International Baccalaureate Organization (IBO)

The IBO is probably the most well recognised of all international curricula. The organisation started in Geneva in 1968 with the IB Diploma, when international educators recognised the need for a global curriculum that allowed transient expatriate families to access a quality education. Since the inception of the diploma programme, the IBO now offers a full school curriculum through the Primary Years Programme and the Middle Years Programme.

Fieldwork Education

As more and more international schools opened, opportunities arose for other agents to enter the market. Fieldwork Education offers programmes for students from age three to fourteen: the International Early Years Curriculum (IEYC), the International Primary Curriculum (IPC) and the International Middle Years Curriculum (IMYC), with the IPC being the most established.

UK-based organisations offering international examinations

Keen to tap into the expanding market of international education, UK-based examination boards started to offer International GCSEs and A-levels. These are not bound by the same regulations that govern schools in England and provide the flexibility that is sought in some international schools. Some of these organisations have changed their names slightly over time, for example, Cambridge International Examinations became Cambridge Assessment International Education. Other international examination boards include OxfordAQA International Qualifications, known as OxfordAQA, and Pearson Edexcel, known as Edexcel.

Of course, some international schools offer the UK examinations and thus receive the protection provided by the UK government in times of crisis. This became apparent during the COVID pandemic, when UK exam boards relaxed the grade boundaries for teacher- and centre-assessed grades.

During 2020, the IBO made no such concessions for their students as can be seen from their published world average for that year. The IB Diploma students of 2020 were essentially penalised by the IBO; their counterparts taking A-levels in 2020 had their grades inflated, while the IB Diploma students in that year did not. After a swift change in leadership, the IBO then accommodated the impact of the pandemic in 2021 in line with UK-based practice.

ASIDE

Does your curriculum meet the design specifications of Dylan Wiliam at the start of this section?

The following has come from the Principals' Training Center.[8] If you answer 'Yes' to any of these statements then your curriculum probably needs attention.

Descriptor	Yes	No
Data from assessments is consistently inconsistent.		
Teachers comment that there is not enough time to complete the curriculum.		
Students consistently fail to reach the expected standard. For example, students do not meet the 'required' level in PE to gain the highest grades.		
Some classes/groups of students fail to achieve the same standard as those in other classes working on the same curriculum.		
Topics are repeated over different years.		
Students are doing different work despite being in the same year.		
Some subjects repeatedly ask for a different timetable structure.		
Teachers use different criteria to assess the type of task.		
Teachers complain of content overload.		
Teachers substitute the school's curriculum with topics they prefer.		
There is a culture that allows individual teachers to make decisions about the learning that students will access.		

---

8   The Principals' Training Center. Available at: https://www.theptc.org/

DESTRUCTION

The optimist thinks this is the best of all possible worlds. The pessimist fears it is true.

Robert Oppenheimer

At times, schools are their own worst enemy. There is a responsibility on school leaders to monitor the school's practices and policies continuously to ensure they are constructive rather than destructive.

The introduction of technology in schools rarely goes hand in hand with policy. Once the latest technology is introduced with a few idealised policies, other policies are often appended on an ad hoc basis to manage retrospectively the plethora of issues that arise.

Bring your own device (BYOD) happens regardless of whether or not the school has a policy for it. Policing corridors and classrooms for furtive playing of Fortnite or Spotify's soporific sounds is another headache for already tired and frustrated teachers who often want clarification and confidence that the praxis and policy are matched. Zealous and uber-strict application of restrictive school policies, technology related or not, creates insecure and cold environments.

Schools, parents and students are now becoming alert to the UN Rights of the Child and are talking with each other to create environments that respect all individuals within the community. There are tensions, of course, within school communities that may be unfeasible to resolve; laws in the host country may present immovable barriers and stop change before the debate has begun. However, with an open and pragmatic dialogue, progress can be made even if it simply recognises the current state of play.

DATA DUNDERHEADS

Another egregious element, marginally behind the patrols from the policy police, is a school that blindly follows trends, without critically analysing the latest spin. A good example would be the divisive 'data dunderheads'. All schools use data in some form. How else could we make sense of what we are doing? But how many schools indiscriminately issue 'target' data and communicate some spurious, software-generated 'target' grade to teachers, students or parents or a combination of these groups?

The pernicious use of 'target' grades in some schools, propagated by a burgeoning industry, is fundamentally in opposition to educational research that discusses the limitations of labelling or the much-used concept of a 'growth mindset'. It all comes from a source of good intention; it just happens to be corrosive. How many schools issue report grades that are the same as 'target' grades, which might have some validity if the 'target' grade was the highest possible grade but not otherwise? Or schools whose 'target' grades are ridiculously low and are not changed by the school because this 'target' grade has been spewed out by the software.

Imagine how demoralising it is for a student to be told they have reached their 'target' in a particular subject in their first summative assessment. Or where the 'target' grade is so low and the teachers are afraid to either change it or, in some instances, suppress students' grades so that they do not surpass the targets! This happens through the thoughtless application of supposedly best practice.

'Target' grades should be used in conjunction with other data generated by a school. A good use of 'target' data would be to aggregate the data, triangulate it with other sources of information, and then use the accumulated collective data to analyse trends and identify strengths and weaknesses in student learning.

Other issues can occur when schools attempt to draw conclusions from partial data. The details in Graph 1 below suggest that in the particular school concerned, the Arab students are significantly underperforming. However, when one looks at the historical trends as shown in Graph 2, another picture emerges. It is not the Arab students where there is a historical issue but the British and European students, with 2023 being the exception for the Arab students.

CAT/GCSE Difference by Nationality: 2023

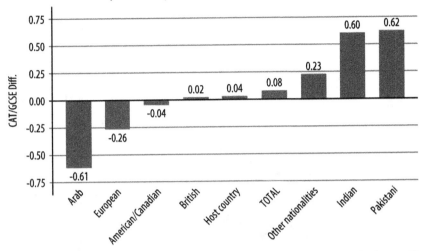

Graph 1: *The difference between the actual (I)GCSE grade and the CAT4 predicted grade for Year 11 students, ranked from lowest to highest for the year 2023. Note that this data is for a single school. Reproduced with the kind permission of the copyright holder.*

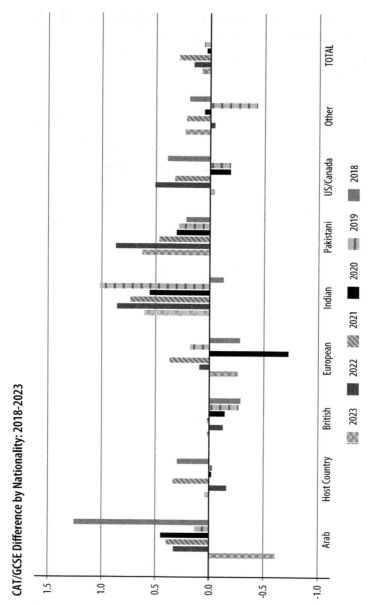

Graph 2: *The difference between the actual (I)GCSE grade and the CAT4 predicted grade for Year 11 students, ordered by nationality for the years 2018–2023. Note that this data is for a single school. Reproduced with the kind permission of the copyright holder.*

We are fortunate to be educators in a time when educational research has a direct impact on learning. Over the past couple of decades, the advancements in research and the introduction of such research into schools have been monumental. Senior leaders just need to be careful in their application of research and how it fits with their student population, particularly when the research may have been carried out with a homogeneous student population that does not represent all schools.

One head recalls that at a school they led in Asia, the students would work tirelessly every day and late into the night as examinations approached and still perform remarkably well in public examinations, despite evidence around the benefits of sleep. This small anecdote demonstrates the critical approach that senior leaders must take when using and applying educational research in an international setting; it does not always translate.

POLICY AMBIGUITY

Badly-worded or ill-thought-through policies create confusion with both staff and students. If a statement on (un)acceptable behaviour is too broad, it begins to lack credibility, and while the intention may be to capture a range of behaviours, it can lead to challenges from belligerent students and parents.

For example, a school had a policy that alcohol was not to be consumed outside or inside the school. Was the school really going to monitor what happened outside the school to this degree? Certainly not, but it caused issues for one head when some parents challenged such a badly-written statement.

In another example, as a sanction for a serious incident that happened outside of school, students were prevented from entering the school to engage with their learning; the school insisted that they learn online from home. The problem was that the school policy did not provide for this sanction, and so the school sought quick approval from the local education authority for an addendum to its policy. This ultimately led to an expensive use of lawyers for both parents and the school in an attempt to resolve the matter. The resulting game of brinkmanship only came to an end because of the fast-approaching school holidays.

Forcing students to sign policies or charters does not set the right tone or encourage a respectful culture that is paramount for learning. Furthermore, these signed documents will not hold up in any resulting legal dispute; it will be evident that the school coerced the students into signing in the first place and most of the students would be under the age of 18. An open discussion about the values contained in the policy or charter is better than a forced signing.

The misuse of social media is at the root of many issues in schools and is an area that attracts much attention. Parents want schools to do things they won't do, such as banning phones. In October 2023, Gillian Keegan, the secretary of state for education in the UK, announced plans for non-statutory guidance for schools to ban mobile phones for the whole school day.[9]

Banning mobile phones in schools will not stop the social media problems; it will transpose them with other issues and the social media storm out of school will still overflow into school life. Students will also utilise their other devices at school to access social media, so the consumption of social media during lessons may increase, rather than decrease, unless of course schools are planning on eradicating all digital devices. An understandable resentment would likely and rightly erupt regarding the hypocrisy of adults using their mobile phones, while students were banned. The international head probably has more leeway than most to adopt a more equitable system. However, as more scholarly research emerges about the use of mobile phones there is clearly a radical adjustment required by all parties concerned: school leaders, teachers, students, parents and governments.

9   BBC News (2023) 'Gillian Keegan pledges crackdown on mobiles in schools'. Available at: https://www.bbc.com/news/uk-66979378

ASIDE

Are any of these school rules or policies familiar?

1. No public displays of affection – to be policed by the prefects.
2. No running at break time – aimed at primary-aged children to keep them safe.
3. A Britishness policy – to emphasise adherence to being 'British' for an international school that had a minority of British families.
4. No high-fives – to make sure there were no unintentional hits.
5. No high grades on a student's first report – because this would not provide room for improvement!

As crazy as some of these sound, they are real examples of policies and procedures in some international schools.

The head should ensure that policies:

*   are aligned with the school's mission, vision and values
*   use simple, unambiguous language; the use of 'must' (compulsory) over 'should' (best practice or a suggestion) is a key distinction
*   address a real issue, not a perceived problem
*   are practical and legally compliant in their enforcement
*   do not try to encompass all scenarios
*   are clear in who has responsibility for the different areas of a policy
*   are written for a particular audience who knows the context.

EXPECTATIONS

We should do everything we can to make sure this country lives up to our children's expectations.

Barack Obama

School leaders are the gatekeepers of standards. Their consistency of application is directly correlated with the culture and climate of the school. An international school leader's role includes the development of a set of standards for all staff that are clearly articulated and consistently implemented across the school.

Setting unattainably high expectations is of no help. Much like some of the negatives associated with a pacesetter leadership style, it can lead to low engagement, stress and feelings of inadequacy among the staff and, consequently, a high staff turnover.

The comparison between teachers setting high expectations and challenges for students, and leaders setting employee expectations is an excellent parallel. Unattainable expectations leave people feeling demotivated, while little challenge results in low growth and no development.

As every school leader knows, students are astute observers of their own learning; they can pinpoint good teaching and suggest ways for their teachers to improve. Expecting and maintaining high standards for teachers translates into high standards for students. And, in the spirit of Obama, leaders should be cognisant of students' expectations of their teachers. Good teachers will already incorporate students' requests about their teaching to aid learning; good leaders will make sure all teachers do the same.

A set of standards, with clear examples of what each standard looks like in practice, will provide the framework for the rest of the staff.

STANDARDS FOR TEACHERS

These teachers' standards have been adapted from guidelines published by the DfE in the UK.[10]

Exceptional expectations

Set high expectations which inspire, motivate and challenge students:

- Set goals that stretch and challenge students of all backgrounds, abilities and dispositions.
- Model consistently the positive attitudes, values and behaviour that are expected of learners.
- Establish a safe and stimulating environment for students, rooted in mutual respect.
- Ensure pastoral work is of the highest possible standard, with a priority on student mental health and wellbeing.

Outstanding outcomes

Promote excellent progress and outcomes by students:

- Be accountable for students' exceptional attainment, progress and outcomes.
- Be aware of and build upon students' capabilities and prior knowledge.
- Guide students to reflect on the progress they have made and their emerging needs.
- Demonstrate knowledge and understanding of how students learn and how this impacts on teaching.
- Encourage students to take a responsible and conscientious attitude to their own work and study.

---

10 *Teachers' standards: Guidance for school leaders, school staff and governing bodies.* (2011). Published by Department for Education, © Crown copyright 2011. Available at: https://www.gov.uk/government/publications/teachers-standards

Curriculum cohesion

Demonstrate excellent subject and curriculum knowledge:

- Have a secure knowledge of the relevant subject(s) and curriculum areas; foster and maintain students' interest in the subject and address misunderstandings.

- Demonstrate a critical understanding of developments in the subject and curriculum areas and promote the value of scholarship.

- Demonstrate an understanding of, and take responsibility for promoting, high standards of literacy, articulacy, oracy and the correct use of English, whatever the teacher's specialist subject or year group.

- Take full responsibility for the continuous development of the curriculum within your team. This includes the vertical and horizontal alignment of knowledge, skills, understandings and dispositions.

- Make significant contributions to, and take full responsibility for, the written curriculum as defined by the school.

- Contribute to the design and provision of an engaging curriculum within the relevant subject area(s) or year group.

Pedagogy and planning

Plan and teach well-structured lessons that meet the needs of all students:

- Impart relevant knowledge, skills and develop students' understanding through highly effective use of lesson time.

- Promote a love of learning and of students' intellectual curiosity.

- Plan collaboratively with colleagues both within one's own subject/ year level and across the school.

- Set homework (where appropriate), plan and contribute to other out-of-class activities to consolidate and extend the knowledge, skills and understanding students have acquired.

- Model the dispositions and values that are reflected in the school's curriculum, mission and vision.

- Continuously reflect systematically on the effectiveness of lessons and approaches to teaching and make adjustments where necessary.
- Use high-quality resources to help students learn and ensure that knowledge is clear and accessible.

Individualised intent

Adapt teaching to respond to the strengths and needs of all students:

- Know when and how to differentiate appropriately, using approaches that enable all students to be taught effectively.
- Have a secure understanding of how a range of factors can inhibit students' ability to learn, and how best to overcome these factors.
- Demonstrate an awareness of, and respond to, the physical, social and intellectual development of children, and know how to adapt teaching to support students' education at different stages of development.
- Have a clear understanding of the needs of all students, including those with additional educational needs, those of high ability, those with English as an additional language and those with disabilities, and be able to use and evaluate distinctive teaching approaches to engage and support them.

Accurate assessment

Make accurate and productive use of assessment:

- Know and understand how to assess the relevant subject and curriculum areas according to the school's assessment policy.
- Make use of formative and summative assessment to secure students' progress.
- Use relevant data to monitor progress, set appropriate targets and plan subsequent lessons.
- Give students regular feedback, both orally and through accurate marking (where appropriate), and encourage students to respond to the feedback.

Respectful relationships

Create a safe and secure environment for all students to flourish. Establish positive relationships with all students based on mutual respect:

- Have clear boundaries and sensible routines in classrooms, and take responsibility for promoting good and courteous behaviour both in classrooms and around the school, in accordance with the school's behaviour policy.

- Create a stimulating and engaging physical space in which students learn.

- Have high expectations of behaviour and establish a framework for discipline with a range of strategies, using praise, sanctions and rewards consistently and fairly, in line with the school's behaviour policy.

- Manage classes effectively, using approaches which are appropriate to students' needs in order to engage and motivate them.

- Maintain excellent relationships with students and act decisively when necessary.

- Treat students with dignity, build relationships rooted in mutual respect, and at all times observe proper boundaries appropriate to a teacher's professional position.

Professional profile

A teacher is expected to demonstrate consistently high standards of personal and professional conduct:

- Make a positive contribution to the wider life and ethos of the school, including being a form tutor, delivering extracurricular activities, contributing during meetings and working collaboratively with colleagues.

- Develop effective professional relationships with colleagues, knowing how and when to draw on advice and specialist support.

- Deploy support staff effectively.

- Take responsibility to improve teaching through appropriate professional development, responding to advice and feedback from colleagues.

- Be fully engaged in the school's professional development portfolio process or its equivalent.
- Communicate effectively with parents with regard to students' achievements and wellbeing.
- Demonstrate respect, celebrate differences and understand the rights of others.
- Maintain a professional regard for the ethos, policies and practices of the school, and set high standards for attendance and punctuality.

STANDARDS FOR LEADERS

As with teachers, it is critical that a school has standards for leaders that can be referenced throughout the year in various conversations and appraisal meetings. The standards below have been adapted from those shared by the Principals' Training Center.[11]

Leadership

Motivate staff to achieve the highest standards, focused around a shared and achievable vision for the school:

- Inspire and motivate staff to achieve the highest standards.
- Galvanise the school community around an achievable mission-driven vision.
- Insist that the main focus is always on student learning and provide leadership on how best to enhance student learning.
- Set goals that stretch and challenge students of all backgrounds, abilities and dispositions.
- Model consistently the positive attitudes, values and behaviour that are expected of learners.
- Establish a safe and stimulating environment for students and staff, rooted in mutual respect.
- Promote a culture of accountability.

---

11   The Principals' Training Center. Available at: https://www.theptc.org/

Professional development

Actively pursue professional development opportunities in order to enhance student learning and personal growth:

- Be alert to the latest pedagogical research, student learning and leadership strategies.
- Facilitate professional learning among colleagues.
- Provide constructive feedback to colleagues to strengthen teaching practice and to improve student learning.
- Provide high-quality learning resources for teachers and students.

Involvement

Participate fully in the life of the school, and demonstrate a positive, collaborative and open approach to challenges and school improvement:

- Develop staff, nurture talent and provide leadership.
- Establish and promote an up-to-date vision.
- Lead and manage teaching and learning.
- Communicate effectively with students, teachers and parents.
- Be visible and involved in the day-to-day life of the school.

Planning

Plan for continual improvement, taking into account the needs of the school community:

- Ensure proper follow-up, through regular monitoring and revision, of the school action plans and policies.
- Ensure there are well-resourced facilities for effective teaching and learning.
- Create an inspiring, collaborative learning environment in which staff and students feel safe and secure.
- Ensure that health and safety regulations are up to date and implemented.

- Provide greater partnership with parents, other learning institutions and career guides.
- Ensure regular revision of staff welfare in terms of salary, health benefits and accommodation.

Values

Model the school's values, as stated in its mission and vision, both in and out of school:

- Possess strong personal virtues and principles which include:
  - inspiration and motivation
  - reliability and honesty
  - equanimity and rationality
  - trust and justice
  - risk taking and innovation
  - a sense of humour.
- Possess the professional skills, qualities and knowledge necessary for the post.
- Maintain ethical practices such as ensuring confidential communication.

Administration

Efficiently and effectively carry out all administrative tasks to the highest standard:

- Be consistent and transparent in all decisions with fair verification and justification of staff issues.
- Set high professional standards and management ethics on administrative tasks and policy making.
- Have a clear sense of direction and aims for the school, according to achievable strategic planning.
- Promote a positive work culture of cooperation, collaboration and communication.

ASIDE

Why don't schools have a common code of conduct for staff and students? In some schools and countries this might be the case, but in many schools there are two levels of accepted behaviour, with students having greater restrictions. Of course, there should be appropriate age-related guidance but the essence should be the same for staff and students, and as the students become older, the expectations should coalesce.

All secondary students could understand and engage with the following points that have been adapted from one of the teacher standards above:

- Impart relevant knowledge and skills, and develop your understanding through highly effective use of lesson time.
- Promote a love of learning and of your intellectual curiosity.
- Learn collaboratively with peers both within one's own class and across other classes in the school.
- Complete homework (where appropriate), plan and contribute to other out-of-class activities to consolidate and extend your knowledge, skills and understanding.
- Model the dispositions and values that are reflected in the school's curriculum, mission and vision.
- Continuously reflect systematically on the effectiveness of lessons and approaches to learning, making adjustments where necessary.
- Develop and use high-quality resources to help your learning and ensure that knowledge is clear and accessible.

How could all the standards above be adapted to include student agency, and one document created that codifies expectations for the entire school community?

FREEDOM

We are faced with the paradoxical fact that education has become one of the chief obstacles to intelligence and freedom of thought.

Bertrand Russell

Leaders of international schools are free to choose from the best educational initiatives around the world, unshackled from the administrative handcuffs of national and state regulations. Yet many international school leaders and governors find themselves resolutely following historical traditions and the patriotic ruts of the marketing gurus.

The hindrance to development and innovation and the lack of cross-pollination of ideas that follows from ploughing the single furrow is self-evident. The best schools are open and outward thinking, ready to critically accept ideas from around the world, even if these ideas emanate from people in countries other than their own. International schools are ideally placed to be at the forefront of innovation in education.

The advantage that some international schools have when compared with their national counterparts is the freedom from tight governmental regulations. At times, the host country's government does play a role in the operations of an international school with varying degrees of success. International schools often find themselves with much autonomy, only held back by senior leaders who have a lack of engagement, a lack of interest or a fear of change.

In England, against a backdrop of increased academisation of schools where the market places an emphasis on results, compounded by government measures that bleed the last drop of creativity from teachers, it is not surprising that more and more teachers are turning to international education.

ISC Research[12] estimates that in the next 10 years, the number of international schools will increase from just over 9000 to more than 16,000 schools. This would require almost 500,000 more teachers. The strongest growth is predicted to be in the British brand of (I)GCSEs. For many British trained teachers, international education serves as a release valve from the pressures of British classrooms; a way for teachers to stay in teaching, refresh their mojo and enjoy a much higher quality of life.

RECRUITMENT

International leaders need to plan for this expansion as recruitment becomes ever more challenging. Training and upskilling local and expatriate staff has already become an effective way for international schools to source the people they need, diversify their staff and meet their ever-growing demands. The safeguarding section later in this book discusses the vigilance that many international schools adhere to when recruiting staff, something that may come as a surprise to some national heads. At a conference, an international colleague of mine was once asked, in all seriousness, by a headteacher from a national school, 'Do you do safeguarding?'

There is a great freedom in recruitment available to international schools, but how many utilise this opportunity? Heads could use their freedom to appoint diverse and high-quality teachers from across the globe. However, we should expect the same outcomes if we persist in following the same processes and advertising in the same way. With a diluted field of applicants due to the expanding market, international heads will have to be far more creative in their recruitment. Perhaps utilising 'lecture-style' lessons, or lessons where students are in multiple classrooms being taught online by a teacher in a different room or even a different country. One thing that schools will need to manage carefully is creating opportunities for flexible working for teachers, as is the expectation from an increasing number of employees.

---

12   ISC Research. Available at: https://iscresearch.com/

The direction of travel, though, is bidirectional. International teachers often return to the UK better prepared, with new ideas and possessing renewed energy. Even if teachers do not return to the UK, they are part of the larger international education sector worth £20 billion to the UK economy (at the last estimate from the DfE in 2015).

However, some UK national teachers are finding it difficult to return to the UK to teach, as if being overseas for a few years has resulted in a lack of development and stunted growth for the teacher. This is where the astute head will consciously connect their school to the current practices in the UK in supporting references that they write. Of course, to do this, the international leader must stay up to date with all current practices. This is a tall order, but with the right networks it is possible.

NETWORKS

International schools have created strong networks across the globe. Like all dynamic institutions, international schools evolve to survive. Various organisations have been created by international school leaders to support and guide schools along their own learning journey.

The Council of International Schools (CIS) provides an accreditation framework for international schools. The New England Association of Schools and Colleges (NEASC) provides a similar service for international and American schools. The DfE has approved a set of standards for British Schools Overseas (BSO) that reflects the current educational and political situation in the UK.

Until recently, the BSO standards required adherence to political dogma that some international schools could not achieve without breaking the laws of the host country. Thankfully, these issues are now resolved and common sense prevails.

Despite the global nature of international education, silos are still created. American- and British-focused schools have their distinct and separate networks; the International Baccalaureate has its own and provides a small bridge between the American and British camps.

REPORTS

Since time is our most precious resource, why do we spend hundreds of hours writing reports for parents who are predominantly interested in grades? It may be an unfair characterisation of some parents but many parents comment that they enjoy meeting teachers to find out details of their son or daughter's learning and look at reports for a summative grade.

Even though the purposeful process of learning has progressed significantly over the past generation, many schools are still wedded to traditional reporting structures. A quick calculation shows that a school with 500 students, each student having an average of eight discrete comments and with a teacher spending an average of five minutes per comment, results in over 300 hours of work; and this is without the elaborate, multi-level checking process in which a lucky few leaders get to partake. Instead, we should report on learning as it happens and provide summative grades to students and parents as and when they are available. This would be a continuous, two-way communication that serves everyone's needs.

AIM HIGH, WORK SMART AND CARE DEEPLY

All international school leaders should aim high, work smart and care deeply; this is a modification of a quote from Hillary Clinton when she was on the campaign trail in the 2016 US presidential election. It encapsulates much of what we endeavour to do in schools and, like Clinton, we probably fall short, just a little; we may not quite create the perfect lesson or the dynamic curriculum that engages all learners. The important thing is to keep going; to demonstrate to the community that we care and that we are striving to aim high, work smart and care deeply.

ASIDE

Mass education is hierarchical in its construction; students have few rights and freedoms. Accepting a place in a school means accepting the school's rules and regulations, but how can schools maintain structure and order while promoting a more equitable learning environment?

Many international schools with a UK connection use the term 'pupil' to reference their learners, regardless of their age. 'Pupil' is very culturally specific to the UK and, due to its origins, positions young people as being subservient to the teacher. Why do so many UK-connected international schools still insist on using the term? A more inclusive term would be 'student' or 'learner', with the latter becoming increasingly popular in schools.

There are great freedoms in international schools. How could the head prove Bertrand Russell wrong by creating a school where freedom of thought is nurtured and celebrated; where intelligence is palpable?

GRIT

... grit grows as we figure out our life philosophy, learn to dust ourselves off after rejection and disappointment, and learn to tell the difference between low-level goals that should be abandoned quickly and higher-level goals that demand more tenacity.

Angela Duckworth

Grit is both a requirement and a nuisance for international school leaders.

Grit is the small stone in the shoe that starts off as a minor annoyance but gradually becomes more and more of a focus, until it is unbearable. As you continue on your journey, it becomes all consuming, especially if it has been joined by some of its friends. Eventually, you find a place to stop, but have you stopped soon enough or is the damage done? Will it require some focused attention to repair the throbbing sore?

How much damage is done depends on how quickly one acts. Act quickly and you can get on your way with a minor indentation that quickly fades; leave it for longer and lasting damage may be done. If you wait until you are in real pain, then it is not just a matter of the initial stone but the collection of rocks that have taken residence in your shoe, some embedding themselves into your epidermis. This requires serious interventions.

If a leader lets issues build then they will face existential challenges. A colleague of mine was employed to 'save' an international school. In his first half-term, over 20 students were expelled: some for racially motivated fighting, some for using weapons, another for hitting a teacher on the head with a hard object. A parent had to be removed from a town hall meeting. The colleague has recently employed a teacher who has taught in prisons.

These kinds of interventions are extreme in most schools, and very rare in international schools, but it does demonstrate the scenarios that can arise if grit is allowed to build. Whether it relates to staff or students, dealing with issues promptly, fairly and consistently is a prerequisite for maintaining the harmonious balance that exists in most international schools. The same head is now facing lawsuits against the school related to the expulsions, and all this before the end of their first term! Clearly the grit at this school had punctured the epidermis.

Schools are not like other workplaces. Dealing with children and young people takes a certain kind of adult; one who can lead and manage in a particular way. The key performance indicators (KPIs) of teachers and school leaders should be that school leavers are articulate, compassionate, courageous young adults with a life-long love of learning, a strong sense of social responsibility and the confidence to engage with the world. Not many places of work can have such altruistic ideals.

But how many schools stop students attending a graduation ceremony because they do not possess these characteristics? How many schools graduate obnoxious and arrogant individuals? And which leaders hold teachers to account for failing to instil a sense of social responsibility into their students?

TOXICITY

The worst kinds of behaviour in organisations are toxic. Peterson and Deal's[13] seminal book addresses multiple dimensions of school culture and is an authoritative reference for all heads when creating and managing school culture. They note that toxic cultures are 'places where negativity dominates conversations, interactions, and planning; where the only stories recounted are of failure.'

---

13   Deal, T.E. and Peterson, K.D. (1999) *Shaping School Culture: The Heart of Leadership*. San Francisco: Jossey-Bass.

Gruenert and Whitaker[14] cite toxicity as one of the most difficult problems faced by school leaders in the process of implementing reform. Toxic behaviour is incredibly hard to detect but once such a culture takes hold, the roots run deep. Gruenert and Whitaker state that a toxic teacher leads other teachers into a collective mindset of:

- Disloyalty to the school mission.
- Irreverence for students and parents.
- A posture of self-defense whenever improvement is mentioned.

Unlike negative teachers, toxic teachers are committed only to themselves and to surviving the next new idea or initiative. Toxic teachers have a spiteful mindset, whispering in others' ears throughout the school and community that the only way to survive this miserable place is to join their gang.

Tackling toxicity

By far the most effective way to tackle toxicity in the workplace is to tackle it directly, and only when it has been witnessed first hand by the person having the conversation. Reward the right adult behaviours and have professional conversations about expectations.

Another way to steer clear of toxicity is to create a shared sense of purpose, with rituals and traditions that celebrate student accomplishment, teacher innovation and parental commitment.

One of the more difficult aspects will be to allow students to hold adults accountable for the shared values that the school espouses. How many staff raise their voices to a disruptive class even though only a few students are causing a disturbance? How many staff make a conscious decision to welcome both students and staff into the school each morning, regardless of past history and relationships.

---

14 Gruenert, S. and Whitaker, T. (2019) *Committing to the Culture: How Leaders can Create and Sustain Positive Schools.* Alexandria, Virginia: ASCD.

Maximise the joy of learning, celebrate connections and establish norms of behaviour for all within the school. The norms of behaviour at St Christopher's School, Bahrain, are shown below.

ASSUME POSITIVE INTENTIONS!

GRIT'S BRIGHTER SIDE

A school leader requires an abundance of grit. The ability to continue to lead in a positive manner when faced with complex and challenging scenarios is integral to such an outward-facing role. The nuanced differences between grit, determination and resilience are important. Grit is often referenced over longer time periods and encompasses sustained determination to achieve a passion.

All leaders will face challenges that really push their comfort envelopes. It is imperative that a school leader has the grit to navigate these difficult occasions, or they will become isolated and eventually redundant.

Much has been written about the need for leaders to have a high degree of empathy for others. The combination of 'grit' and 'empathy' in leaders is an interesting juxtaposition.

Can a leader possess grit and not be empathetic? Perhaps it is possible, however being conscious over an extended period of time of the complex issues one is dealing with normally requires a level of self-awareness and empathy for others. A leader with high grit and low empathy is someone who doesn't care what others think about their leadership, someone who ploughs on until they bulldoze their way out of the school. In contrast, leaders possessing both grit and empathy will provide the combination that establishes strong leadership in the most challenging of circumstances.

ASIDE

Which is more important: intellectual ability or hard work and grit? Over time, it is possible to develop talent in a variety of leadership skills through the consistency of grit and effort in all aspects of one's professional life. It is of little use to intellectualise about a particular strategy if one does not possess the determination to acquire the skills needed to action a well-thought-through strategy.

To develop grit:

- be passionate about your vision for the school
- give your utmost to the vision, perhaps breaking it down into shorter-term, achievable goals
- recognise your low points and discover what is required to lift yourself during these moments in time; don't expect others to help
- nourish the optimism that you felt at various stages along the journey.

HARMONY

... intimate beauty ... comes from the harmonious order of its parts ...

Henri Poincaré

Harmony is an excellent way to describe the goal for international heads; to create a culture and climate where different groups can learn together without purposefully wishing harm to others.

Cultural difference is probably the key concept that runs through many international schools, and it is the harnessing and cultivation of these differences that makes leading an international school so fascinating. Hofstede's[15] work on culture provides a way in which cultural differences may be analysed. He originally started with four cultural dimensions that has since been amended to six.

- Individualistic/collectivist – how personal needs are prioritised compared to the needs of the group.
- Masculine/feminine – the differences in whether groups place a higher value on achievement or nurture.
- High/low uncertainty avoidance – a group's tolerance for ambiguity, uncertainty and change.
- High/low power distance – the extent to which the less powerful members of a group accept and expect that power is distributed unequally.

---

15 Hofstede, G. (2011) 'Dimensionalizing cultures: The Hofstede model in context'. *Online Readings in Psychology and Culture.* **2**(1).

- Long term vs short term – whether the values of the group have a long- or short-term orientation.
- High/low indulgent – the degree to which the group values freedoms.

International school leaders may use Hofstede's framework to analyse their leadership team's cultural dimensions and compare them to the dominant cultures of the school community. For example, if the senior leaders in the school all come from individualistic, masculine societies, yet the majority of the school population – teachers and students – comes from a high-power distance society, there will be tensions.

CULTURE, CULTURE, CULTURE

In the student populations of some international schools there are mixed and changing demographics. ISC Research charts the changing communities with more and more local families using the services of international schools as a way to increase their social and economic mobility.

This may lead the international school leader to decide which local celebrations they will observe and which ones they will not. If a school has not previously celebrated a local tradition or religious event, to start to do so may strain the community, especially if it means changing the structure of the day. However, with changing demographics, this is just one of the many decisions international heads face.

In these instances, the mission and vision of the school are important anchors, as is a belief in what is right, to create a timely and comprehensive community communication plan. The emotive concerns around cultural changes should not be underestimated. One school head, noting the increased number of Muslim students in the school, changed the school's timings slightly for a period of a few days during Ramadan and subsequently received some shocking messages from parents:

> This is a Christian school. Why should we change [what we do] for Ramadan timings? We should stick to being Christian.
>
> If you want to fast and be a good Muslim, go to [another school named].

While such complaints are small in number, they may be frequent. But through careful planning and even better communication, leaders can make a good attempt to manage the intricacies of culture and climate in an international setting.

An international school leader has to take responsibility for their own cultural literacy.

CREATING CULTURE

School culture exists, and it is the head's job to make sure it is the culture they want. Writing at The Harvard Graduate School of Education, Shafer summarises the following elements as being significant characteristics of a good culture in schools.[16]

- Fundamental beliefs and assumptions, or the things that people at your school consider to be true. 'All students have the potential to succeed' or 'Teaching is a team sport'.

- Shared values, or the judgements people at your school make about those beliefs and assumptions – whether they are right or wrong, good or bad, just or unjust. 'Teachers should collaborate with colleagues.'

- Norms: how members believe they should act and behave or what they think is expected of them. 'Everyone should make at least one contribution during team meetings.'

- Patterns and behaviours, or the way people actually act and behave in your school. 'There is active participation at weekly meetings.'

- Tangible evidence, or the physical, visual, auditory or other sensory signs that demonstrate the behaviours of the people in your school. 'Car parks fill up very early in the morning.'

Bandura[17] from Stanford University uncovered that a group's belief in itself was associated with greater success. This has since been confirmed by different researchers in various domains. Bandura called this

---

16   Shafer, L. (2018) 'What makes a good school culture?' Available at: https://www.gse. harvard.edu/news/uk/18/07/what-makes-good-school-culture
17   Bandura, A. (1997) *Self-efficacy: The Exercise of Control.* New York: W.H. Freeman and Company, p. 477.

'collective efficacy'. John Hattie[18] has placed collective efficacy as the top factor influencing student outcomes, with its impact being significant.

For this reason alone, heads should be consciously encouraging a culture of collective responsibility and understanding around the idea that a shared belief in the efficacy of the team will improve student learning. It is one of the characteristics of a good culture in schools, where the team believes in its collective agency.

The transient nature of teachers in some international schools makes this a priority for heads, as they focus on sustaining the 'collective efficacy' of staff year on year.

CONTRASTING CULTURES

Hinde[19] comments that 'teachers work within a cultural context that influences every aspect of their pedagogy, yet this pervasive element of schools is elusive and difficult to define'. According to Deal and Peterson[20] culture is 'the glue, the hope, and the faith that holds people together'.

A well-thought-through strategic plan for parent communications and engagement should be part of this glue. As aspirational parents from the host country utilise international schools to provide (supposedly) better opportunities for their children, leaders need to be mindful of this context as they construct their inclusive messaging.

For Hofstede et al.[21], successful intercultural communication is dependent upon three factors.

1. Awareness – a recognition that we each carry a mental software which is different to that carried by others.

---

18 Hattie, J. (2016, July) *Mindframes and maximizers*. 3rd Annual Visible Learning Conference held in Washington, DC.
19 Hinde, E.R. (2004) 'School culture and change: An examination of the effects of school culture on the process of change'. Available at: https://www.researchgate.net/publication/251297989_School_Culture_and_Change_An_Examination_of_the_Effects_of_School_Culture_on_the_Process_of_Change
20 Deal, T.E. and Peterson, K.D. (1999) *Shaping School Culture: The Heart of Leadership*. San Francisco: Jossey-Bass.
21 Hofstede, G., Hofstede, G.J. and Minkov, M. (2010) *Cultures and Organizations: Software of the Mind*. 3rd ed. London: McGraw Hill.

2. Knowledge – learning about the symbols, heroes, rituals and values of other cultures.

3. Skills – recognising and applying the symbols, recognition of heroes and practising rituals by getting along and fitting in.

Being mindful of Hofstede's factors above, and the mix of transient expatriate families and aspirational host families, and multiple nationalities among staff, a nuanced communication plan and different types of engagement could be organised.

International heads need to learn quickly how to decode facial expressions and tones of voice, whether to make eye contact, and how to convey emotions in conversations with many different ethnic groups. One faux pas may be forgiven, but rarely is a second chance allowed.

Expatriate families may be well versed in international schools, and may be more transactional in their interactions. In contrast, host families may be more invested in the international school and expect to see significant improvements in all aspects of a school's operations and learning over their time with the school. This presents a dichotomy for international school leaders: to change or not to change? Expatriate families who are with a school for a few years rarely want their own child to experience significant change where the outcomes are far from certain and may not impact their own children.

Of course, all leaders wish to make improvements, so the messaging around change in the international school context should be cognisant of the competing tensions between groups within the parent population.

Both groups – host families and expatriate families – require practical details about their child's education, which are relatively easy to provide. However, with many host families investing in an education that provides global economic opportunities for their children, while also looking for a change in their own social mobility, these high expectations require far more connected communication.

And all this takes place in an increasingly competitive international school market, where schools vie for space, and the messaging war of marketing executives, making claims that the school may not be able to meet, creates contradictions that the head must manage.

The following story provides an excellent example of contrasting cultures. A headteacher of an international school in the Middle East planned to deliver a professional development session on pedagogy. They discussed the format of the session with their deputy head, a local Arab, who politely asked whether refreshments would be offered as the session was due to last two hours after school. The head replied, 'of course'. Up to this point, the head's experience had been in a British international school setting where the majority of colleagues were from the UK, so they were expecting tea, coffee and biscuits. About an hour before the session was to begin, the head saw a strange commotion and rushed over to see if everything was fine, only to find a full buffet with two whole lambs being brought into the hall. The head called their colleague to ask him 'have we booked the wrong venue?' to which the reply was 'No, you said we could have refreshments so we brought lunch!' Needless to say, the afternoon of professional development was very well received, with a full four-course meal!

STAYING ON MESSAGE

Schools have evolved over time and methods of communicating do not always keep up with the latest technology. Most parents now use social media and their phone for all their communications needs. It is, therefore, essential that schools provide timely, concise messages, accessible on a mobile phone, that are simple to understand with a clear call to action.

In some schools there is still a weekly or monthly antiquated letter from the head; it often sprawls over two or three pages of headed paper and can be filled with self-reflections from an outsized ego. Schools may believe that by emailing this to parents, they are staying up to date and relevant, but many parents now use Tik Tok as their go-to service for all sorts of information.

Schools need to adapt quickly or they will disappear.

ASIDE

Part of creating harmony in a school is being optimistic as a leader and ensuring that the school has a sense of optimism for the future. Heads need to feel optimistic about their own future, so that they can be optimistic about that of the school.

Harmony may be thought of as the level of cooperation between people, the absence of disagreement, the manner in which conflict is managed or a combination of these and other factors.

How would you define a harmonious school?

Is it all 'touchy feely' or is there a systematic way to achieve harmony?

Wong[22] mentions that social harmony in the East is about how disagreements are settled in a peaceful manner. While schools will have a grievance policy or similar with much detail about the procedures to follow as the disagreement escalates:

- How much effort and thought are put into managing disagreements peacefully?
- Are there as many pages in the grievance policy on how to resolve conflicts amicably as there are about how the conflict will escalate?

22   Wong, C.K. (2009) 'Comparing social quality and social harmony from a governance perspective'. *Development and Society.* **38**(2): pp. 237–257.

INNOVATIONS

Innovation is the ability to see change as an opportunity – not a threat.

Steve Jobs

Much of the work of an international school senior leader involves staying present in the education debate and ensuring the school they are leading is pushing the educational envelope. Schools must innovate. As I write, generative artificial intelligence (AI) recently exploded into the mainstream with ChatGPT, Bing and Gemini; AI tools that are becoming firmly embedded in our digital ecosystem.

The San Francisco-based company OpenAI, founded in 2015, released ChatGPT in November 2022 and, reportedly achieved over one million users in less than a week. Education conferences are awash with the impact of AI on learning; the familiar mantra that students will not require any knowledge is being regurgitated, much as it was shortly after Google's launch in 1998.

It is the senior leader's responsibility to stay abreast of new innovations and developments and keep the school in the educational moment.

Since the advent of mass schooling in the early 19th century, the focus on education has been a utilitarian approach, creating individuals who will be able to contribute meaningfully, in the economic sense, to society. This is essentially the same today. The sense of exploration and the sheer joy of expanding one's intellect within philosophical frameworks has been lost in mass schooling. Of course, there are a few schools that strive for a true holistic education that encompasses the purposeful development of character and intellect across disciplines within a historical context, while also succeeding very well at jumping through the various circus hoops called examinations.

It is incumbent on school leaders, now more than ever, to consider deeply the purpose of education in the context of AI. According to ChatGPT, at the time of writing, the purpose of education is:

> ... multi-faceted and can vary depending on the context and goals of the individuals and societies involved. However, some of the primary purposes of education are:
>
> 1. Personal development: Education can help individuals develop their knowledge, skills and abilities, which can lead to personal growth, fulfilment and success. Education can provide individuals with the tools and resources they need to pursue their passions and achieve their goals.
>
> 2. Socialisation: Education can also serve as a means of socialisation, helping individuals to learn about their society and culture and to develop a sense of shared values and identity. Through education, individuals can learn to understand and respect others' perspectives and ways of life, promoting social cohesion and harmony.
>
> 3. Economic development: Education can play a crucial role in promoting economic development, by providing individuals with the knowledge and skills needed to succeed in the workforce. By developing a skilled and educated workforce, education can drive innovation, productivity and economic growth.
>
> 4. Citizenship: Education can help individuals to become informed and active citizens, with a deep understanding of their rights and responsibilities, and the ability to participate effectively in the democratic process. Education can foster critical thinking, problem-solving and decision-making skills, which are essential for effective citizenship.
>
> 5. Cultural preservation: Education can also serve as a means of preserving cultural heritage and traditions, by providing individuals with the knowledge and skills needed to understand and appreciate their culture and history. By promoting

cultural awareness and understanding, education can help to preserve and celebrate the diversity of human experience.

In summary, the purpose of education is multifaceted and can encompass personal development, socialisation, economic development, citizenship and cultural preservation. By promoting these goals, education can contribute to individual and societal growth and success, and promote social, economic and cultural progress.

With better prompts and further refinement, I am sure ChatGPT and its successors could create a more sophisticated response. However, its current attempt is satisfactory at best.

KNOWLEDGE IN THE TIME OF AI

The nuanced understanding about using AI in its current form is that the output is dependent on the input. And the input is dependent upon a person's current knowledge. Students cannot refine a prompt or ask better questions without a broad and sophisticated knowledge base to draw upon. Once a response is generated from AI, the output will require critical analysis. The scope for fake information to be propagated as fact, left unchecked because the user has no reference points except AI tools, is deeply worrying.

The physiological process of learning has not changed significantly over the past millennium. External information is stored first in one's working memory. It is then transferred to short-term memory from where it is either lost or hard-wired into long-term memory. Through this process, information becomes useful knowledge that may be synthesised and used to create new knowledge.

The key part here is that the cognitive processes within each individual are similar. AI will not, at this stage, change these processes. What AI may do is become a significant environmental input, taking the place of traditional methods of learning facilitation.

It is, therefore, with urgency that school leaders need to clarify the effective use of AI in learning and, following Job's comment, seize the opportunity to innovate.

AI could be used to generate answers that must be analysed critically by students, picked to pieces and re-assembled with their own and their teacher's knowledge to form a better paragraph or a more sophisticated essay. AI could be used to mark and annotate essays automatically. At St Christopher's School, Bahrain, a computer science teacher has developed a system that uses AI to mark extended-response questions and provide written feedback. No doubt it will not be too long before Google's AI is integrated within their G-Suite for Education platform, along with a plethora of software companies who will drop their unsolicited emails into your inbox.

Consider the Turing Test: 'Can machines think?' Is it possible to differentiate between the responses from a machine and those from a human? Our world is about to be transformed in so many ways, not least by the greater intrusion or inclusion of AI into all of our lives.

How many times have you been fooled by an AI-generated voice or image? What does the future hold? Will there be some kind of symbiotic transference of knowledge from AI to the human brain where the current model of cognitive learning is no longer a valid representation of how we process information? Will neurohacking become the norm and, indeed, be a requirement for successful participation in future societies, where sub-groups of purists who resist technological implants are marginalised?

With these thoughts and questions in mind, it is imperative that school leaders continue to facilitate the joyful acquisition of knowledge, skills, understanding and competencies, using AI as a powerful resource, not as a substitute for knowledge. An emphasis on critical analysis should become the most treasured of attributes; one that should be consciously and constantly refined and finessed in the context of AI development.

Geoffrey Hinton, regarded as the godfather of AI, comments:

> It's quite conceivable that humanity is a passing phase in the evolution of intelligence.

And to (mis)quote Confucius:

> By three methods we may learn: first, by reflection, which is noblest; second, by imitation, which is easiest; and third by experience, which is the bitterest.

AI has the power to harness all three methods, but which ones will we utilise in schools?

ASIDE

'Do what you love. Passion is everything. Innovation doesn't happen without it. Dig deep to identify your true passion.' Steve Jobs was not passionate about computers; he was passionate about building tools to help people unleash their potential. One of the most profound remarks Jobs ever made occurred at the end of one of his last major public presentations. Jobs said, 'It's the intersection of technology and liberal arts that makes our hearts sing.'[23]

Ask yourself, 'What makes your heart sing?' Follow the answer.

Schools have a responsibility to engage with the concept of innovation. First to instil a sense of innovation in the students, through the curriculum design and by enabling curious students to question everything. Secondly, as an organisation that itself innovates, that demonstrates what innovation looks like, so that students and staff experience this first hand.

How could a teacher, a senior leader or a head support students to innovate?

---

23   Gallo, C. (2014) 'The 7 innovation secrets of Steve Jobs'. Forbes. Available at: https://www.forbes.com/sites/carminegallo/2014/05/02/the-7-innovation-secrets-of-steve-jobs/?sh=582a0872751c

JABBERWOCKERY

'And hast thou slain the Jabberwock?
Come to my arms, my beamish boy!
O frabjous day! Callooh! Callay!'
He chortled in his joy.

Lewis Carroll

The nonsense poem of Lewis Carroll provides the perfect metaphor for the plethora of puerile issues that senior school leaders must deal with, sometimes on a daily basis. Whether it is to disentangle the utter mess and carnage that has ensued from a badly-thought-through procedure (never one's own, of course) or an obtuse disagreement between two mediocre teachers, a senior school leader must normally make the final decision that might be to kill the process or even end the contract of a teacher.

School leaders spend much of their time dealing with other people's nonsense. Student disagreements are often the easiest to manage, as restorative processes and young, open minds all aid healing. In contrast, parents and staff demand a disproportionate amount of time from school leaders. In international schools, cultural differences play an even larger part in these disagreements, which may present as unreasonable expectations from entitled parents or staff. Disentangling such issues from cultural norms may take time and patience, and might even be impossible.

Where the international school is based will determine the issues that arise. In countries where education is highly valued, parents may be deferential or may interact in a particular way. A leader may first have to decode the meaning of the interaction and then behave in a way that may be alien to their own internalised communication processes.

A wise head will not dismiss the good intentions of a parent. It is necessary to distil the best from parent complaints, suggestions or ideas. Many international school parents are highly intelligent, with high-pressure jobs that demand the best from people. Some parents work in education themselves. However, I have encountered staff at some international schools who will dismiss all parents as interfering, with the refrain: 'Let us do our job, we are the professionals.'

In some cases, the schools may be right, but they are not right all of the time. Using qualifications as a proxy for intelligence, the parent body of an international school probably possesses far more impressive qualifications than those of the staff working in the school. Yes, the staff have experience, but experience alone does not bring wisdom.

STUDENTS

Except for the universal problems that arise, students do not really create much nonsense for the head to manage, regardless of the country. But there are important differences that arise when students from a different culture enter an international school for the first time.

Students who come from a culture different from that of the school may seem impervious to suggestions, they may not ask for clarification in their understanding and, in certain cases, they may even demand respect from students younger than themselves. Some may find open-ended class investigations too difficult at the start of their time in a new international school. Cooperative learning strategies that the teacher is confident in using may be alien to new students, who might be more comfortable with rote learning.

It is these type of cultural differences that often clash with the predominant culture of the school. This is where an alert senior leader will structure particular support and discuss pedagogical expectations with staff. Hofstede's framework on cultural dimensions, mentioned in the section on Harmony, could be applied to the student body to determine areas of cultural dissonance.

Ensuring that students are assimilated into the culture of the school is a priority for student success. It does not mean neglecting their own rich culture but helping them function as they navigate the complex and alien interactions within their new community. Having an inclusive culture is part of this process.

Managing additional support for English language learning or particular educational requirements in a country that has no national provision or structure for supporting students with educational needs, other than marginalising them, is very demanding.

In one country, a head recalls that students who were deemed to require additional support had their national identification card labelled 'retard'. Unsurprisingly, the country did not have many students receiving additional educational support and there was no national infrastructure in place. International school leaders will need to put in place practices that utilise the best from a country's support services, but it may be necessary for families to access expertise outside the host country of the school.

STAFF

International teachers are far more savvy than their earlier counterparts who led the way in international teaching. Knowledge of rights and responsibilities in reference to the local labour law, comparison of remuneration packages between schools and the use of lawyers are all part and parcel of the international educator. A common request from international teachers is for a leave of absence.

Leave of absence

Schools need to strike the right balance when it comes to leave for international staff. It will be different in different settings. One view would be that international staff have signed up for life overseas and that this may mean missing a wedding or a special birthday because it is impossible to travel back home without needing time off school. Another, more sympathetic, perspective is that staff are away from their country of origin and that policies should be created to support limited absence.

Whatever position a school leader takes, it must be applied fairly and consistently, no matter how much a particular staff member gives, or does not give, to the school. In some instances, policies are so embedded that it is virtually impossible to change practices without a major volcano erupting.

In one school with a generous level of compassionate leave (granted at the head's discretion), a staff member, who had already travelled overseas, put in a second request for leave. Their relative had recently died and the staff member took it upon themselves to interpret and award themselves the maximum level stipulated in the policy's entitlement. Needless to say, this was addressed.

In another example, a staff member asked for leave to attend a concert in another country, citing wellbeing issues. Policies and practices can be abused by the occasional staff member.

And then, of course, there are the examples where staff phone in sick or absent themselves; the last day of term being a prime time for a few errant laggards. One head references a staff member who posted a social media photograph of themselves in the airport business lounge, sipping champagne at 10am in the morning, on the last day of term.

Many schools do have special days that staff members can take off, either wellbeing days or something similar. But with the current emphasis on wellbeing and mental health provision, what is the right balance of support for staff versus the education of children? This is a debate that should often be had and the particular policy updated regularly and communicated to staff.

Some of the areas where staff members may take time off in addition to the standard leave entitlements include: maternity leave, rest period entitlement for breastfeeding, paternity leave, compassionate leave, parental leave for child sickness or to attend a school event, discretionary leave or emergency leave.

The application of policy to leave requests is one of the most contentious issues in international schools. When a staff member is refused leave, there will invariably be a similar case where leave was previously granted for a different colleague. It builds resentment if not handled carefully and consistently.

The head is the fulcrum in these decisions, balancing staff wellbeing and school culture on one side with student education on the other.

PARENTS

Occasionally, parental requests or demands impinge on the head's time, sometimes, too frequently.

Some parents may have little tolerance for innovation and for the school to be seen as an institution that is itself learning, especially if they are on a three-year assignment and do not want their child to be part of an 'experiment' being conducted by the forward-looking school.

The international parent may have a strong history with travel and international schools, or it may be their inaugural sojourn into the wilds of the world. Both types of parent have much to offer a school, while both can equally provide their own headaches.

The experienced international parent will bring ideas and energy, becoming a strong member of the community. Alternatively, they may harness their energy as a force against the school, particularly if they have personal issues or feel wronged by the school. Some parents are third-culture kids themselves and will bring this additional perspective into the mix, reminiscing about their own experiences when international education was in its infancy and the proportion of host families was much smaller.

In contrast, the newly minted expatriate parent may be anxious about the move, may constantly question the expertise of the staff and the leadership as their beliefs may be rooted in ignorance or fear about the standard of the education provided. The degree of resistance is often related to the agency which the parent(s) felt when moving. The astute leader will recognise these issues and be able to affirm and support the new parents until they recognise the quality of education on offer.

Parents who move abroad for the first time, with one of them having a senior position in a company with much disposable income, may take time to adjust to their new standing in the community. This vaunted position of wealth and prestige may bring an arrogance that translates into aggressive or rude communication with the school. Demanding meetings, belittling teachers or sending email messages that verge on the abusive are, sadly, common traits that too many leaders have to deal with in schools.

As the demographic shift continues from expatriate families to local families, so too do the issues. Respecting the values of the host nation is essential, yet cultural differences can be huge. In more than one country, corporal punishment is accepted in schools, although there was a media outcry when a teacher in a local school killed a student with a rattan cane. Sadly, the practice of using a rattan still persists.

Some parents will always see the relationship with the school as being transactional. The degree to which this is tolerated is up to the head. Of course, there is a transactional element, but the best education is about establishing strong partnerships with the home and this can only be done through a degree of trust, and through honest and empathetic communication.

ASIDE

Measuring amorphous entities like culture and climate is notoriously difficult, but there are external consultants who make various claims about their ability to measure culture. The head will need to ascertain which work for their particular context. One company that the author has used is Brands with Values, who claim to be able to provide an authentic map of the organisation's culture and its people.

Whatever a head does, gathering meaningful data is useful to be able to focus attention to reduce the Jabberwockery in the school.

KNOWLEDGE

Learning how to learn used to be an optional extra in education; today, it's a survival skill.

Dylan Wiliam

Knowledge in all its spectral versions provides colour and character for a leader.

Knowledge of oneself as a leader allows for easier decision-making and clearer communication. There are many decisions that a leader makes in a day; some will be easy but most require a degree of reflection and, potentially, adaptive leadership skills. It is this self-knowledge that will prepare a leader for the toughest decisions, where a judgement, often based on values, principles or beliefs, will be required.

On these occasions it might be better to follow Angela Merkel's leadership style … and wait a little. Waiting provides time for the issue to manifest itself properly. It provides thinking and meeting time to fully understand the context and the various outcomes that are possible. It gives the leader time to take a different perspective. It does not stop a decision being made, but in these value-based decisions, it gives the other parties time to reflect, too, and perhaps assimilate some of the more nuanced details that have been shared in the meantime.

Staying up to date with global educational trends should be part of a head's contract. It is easy in international schools to become an island and inward looking. This is where professional networks play an integral role.

LEGAL CONTEXT

As an international school head moves between countries, they should quickly assimilate and understand the main aspects of local labour law. For example, what are the responsibilities of employees and employers with respect to sickness, compassionate leave and, importantly, contractual obligations if an employee is not meeting expectations and has capability issues.

Some countries have very clear guidelines if an investigation of an employee is required, particularly if it may lead to dismissal. The most serious of cases might involve designating personnel to particular roles, such as a prosecuting officer, calling witnesses and creating a panel for a hearing. Each country will have their own procedures to follow, so a head should make sure they follow the correct process, otherwise lengthy court cases may ensue. A typical procedure in Malaysia, called a domestic inquiry, is detailed below. The domestic inquiry is modelled on what happens in a court, and is quite different from processes in some other countries.

DOMESTIC INQUIRY

A 'show cause' letter is handed to the employee where the issues are carefully articulated. In some cases, this may be written by a lawyer depending on the severity of the case being considered. In other countries this corresponds to the issuance of a disciplinary letter.

The employee may be suspended if the issue is significant and a guilty outcome might lead to termination of employment. Another reason for suspension would be if the employee's presence at school might reasonably interfere in the process. In all cases suspension is carried out under the country's labour laws.

The employee is required to provide a written response to the 'show cause' letter. At this stage the options are to stop the disciplinary proceedings or proceed to the inquiry. If the inquiry is to proceed the head would need to appoint a panel that consists of senior staff members who will make the final judgement.

The head will also appoint a senior staff member to 'prosecute' the employee. The employer has the right to appoint a staff member as their 'defence'.

Both teams gather their own information and put forward their own arguments. The 'prosecution' and the 'defence' have the right to bring their own witnesses to the inquiry.

If the panel finds the employee guilty then they make a recommendation regarding the disciplinary action to be taken. The head then has the final say.

Most international schools will have a policy based around similar procedures, with different nomenclature.

PROFESSIONAL DEVELOPMENT

Like all staff, senior leaders should be engaged in relevant learning that challenges them and enhances their knowledge. Whether it is about leadership strategies or the particulars of metacognition in the classroom, it is imperative that senior leaders stay abreast of new developments as well as being familiar with the established and accepted understandings in education. In all situations, these understandings should be questioned and refined for contextual use. The story of Gardner's multiple intelligences[24] being misunderstood and incorrectly applied is an excellent example of where heads must be carefully critical of all theories. (I reference the misuse of 'target' grades in the section on Destruction.)

An important aspect for the development of international school leaders is to visit local government schools in order to understand the context of their own growing local student population.

A head should ensure that there are funds available for their own professional development, either through contractual agreements or as part of the annual budget process. The same allocation of funds should be done for attendance at conferences. A head should also

---

24   Gardner, H. (1993) *Frames of Mind: The Theory of Multiple Intelligences*. New York: Basic Books.

support and guide reluctant senior leaders to participate in their own professional development.

KNOWLEDGE OF STAFF

A leader needs to know their staff, and this can only come through direct communication with each and every staff member. It is a task that cannot be delegated. Inevitably leaders will be more relaxed and conversations will flow better with some people than others. A head needs to recognise this and actively seek out the staff members to whom they do not naturally gravitate.

Through the aggregate of these informal conversations with staff, a leader will be able to understand the climate of the school, where the pinch points are and how to frame and time key decisions or changes.

A head should be focused on many things when reviewing their staff. Three key areas are: personal circumstances, professional capabilities and potential for growth.

Personal circumstances

In a school, there will always be staff members who are experiencing difficult issues in their personal lives. It could be a divorce, the loss of a close relative, financial concerns, problems with their teenager. The list is pretty ubiquitous but knowing who among the staff are experiencing these issues will provide opportunities for the head to demonstrate empathy, and offer support. International heads may have to approve a leave of absence. Knowing the details helps support the decision-making process.

If a new teacher has been at a previous, much-loved, school for a long period of time, then it may take a few years for them to settle, if they settle at all. The emotional ties to the previous school remain strong and become sentimental over time. There is little one can do except enquire about how they are managing the transition.

Professional capabilities

Knowing a colleague's professional capacities may come through various channels, especially when a head is new to a school. However, after at most a year, a head should have observed all teachers teach and have met with all staff in the school for an initial conversation.

The head should focus on understanding the professional background, current strengths and areas for development of staff members. Knowing the previous place of employment is sometimes useful as it provides a context for a teacher's approach, particularly if it is different from the current pedagogical expectations.

Potential for growth

A fundamental aspect of a head's responsibility is to develop staff, which can only be done if the head knows their staff. Understanding the career aspirations and managing the alignment between colleagues' expectations and their observed characteristics and abilities may be a tricky conversation that requires astute coaching skills from the senior leader.

ASIDE

How do you manage institutional knowledge? Are there processes in place to capture and share the knowledge that individuals and teams hold? Most schools will have procedures for when staff leave. Do these procedures involve the formal contact of ex-employers for a few years after an employee has left?

Institutional knowledge has little value until it is connected with a strategy. So, the outcomes of knowledge acquisition or the purposeful management of knowledge can only be viewed through a proxy. How many schools actively seek knowledge of the organisation and share it with the relevant staff? In large schools across multiple sites, sharing knowledge is part of ensuring a cohesive culture and consistency in practice.

What investment is made in professional development for staff and how is this new knowledge processed by the school? Is there any action research being undertaken or surveys administered that generate new knowledge? Do the expectations around professional practice create knowledge-sharing opportunities?

LEADERSHIP

Leadership is about making others better as a result of your presence and making sure that impact lasts in your absence.

Sheryl Sandberg

Leadership is about relationships and behaviours, and all the complexities that these bring to life. In an international setting, the interconnectedness of staff is most likely going to be highly conspicuous as staff work and socialise together; staff children will play and fall out of favour with each other. These relationships need to be managed and ring-fenced, kept at arm's length.

It is one aspect of international education that differs significantly from that of day schools in national systems, with international school staff living and socialising together in a way that is reminiscent of college days or working in a boarding school. The difficulty of keeping professional and personal lives separate is a serious business in international schools and one that the international school leader must actively and consciously maintain; both their own friendships and those of the staff they lead.

Other differences between being an international school leader and, say, a school leader in the UK relate to cultural sensitivities. These need to be understood quickly to avoid misunderstandings. For example, the school may trespass on the historical territory of a monkey troop and that will require very careful handling, or it may have to deal with corruption in a way that really strikes at the heart of a leader's moral compass.

Supporting staff in a foreign land is different from employing staff in their home country. It involves significant preparation, from meeting new staff off the plane, to arranging work visas, to providing accommodation with a stocked fridge, a SIM card and, probably, a loan for the first month in the country. In extreme cases, a senior leader may need to support staff who have been incarcerated for something that would not have been an issue in their home country. This is a real issue that occasionally makes the news.

INTEGRITY

An international school leader may find themselves in positions where their principles are challenged. A head in South East Asia recalls the time they were asked by a council official to meet in a car park with a brown envelope of money to avoid a fine for the school. Needless to say, the head didn't attend the meeting and the school paid the fine.

It can also work the other way. A senior leader, having problems with the local rules around refuse collection at their home, kindly left a couple of bottles of beer for the collectors in the hope that they would take an extra bag of refuse that had accumulated over the week. On the day of collection, the leader was dismayed to find two bottles of beer, untouched, and the extra bag of refuse next to the empty bin. Undeterred, the senior leader saw this as a challenge and left six bottles of beer the following week. Undeterred, too, the refuse collectors left the six unopened bottles of beer and the three additional refuse bags that had built up. Panicking, the senior leader put the additional bags of refuse in the car and drove to the local recycling point, knowing full well that the bags were not the approved recycling material. However, when the supervisor was not looking, the senior leader quickly managed to sneak them into a large skip, smiling at the accomplishment. Unbeknown to the senior leader, a conscientious citizen alerted the supervisor to the issue, who promptly stopped the senior leader from leaving and handed back the non-recyclable refuse. Defeated, the senior leader paid the additional fee for the bags of refuse to be taken by the refuse collectors.

Or a more subtle form of corruption where a developer offers the head and their family a stay in a luxury hotel in the hope that the school may work with them in the future. Or a school leader who had to remove a child from their school because two sets of parents had fallen out and one parent had more 'wasta' (clout) than the other. Most school leaders will have stories that push against their principles, and there are certainly many that occur overseas, perhaps because these are more visible to the outsider. The ethical tests of Marc Le Menestrel[25] (a decision scientist at INSEAD) are:

1. The sleeping test: 'If I do this, can I sleep well at night?'

2. The newspaper test: 'If it wouldn't look right on the front page of your daily newspaper, it probably isn't quite right.'

3. The mirror test: 'If I do this, can I feel comfortable with myself when facing my mirror?'

4. The teenager test: 'If I do this, would I mind telling my 16-year-old son about it?'

These four tests perfectly encapsulate the types of dilemma that leaders face on a regular basis. Tests 2 and 4 involve hypothetical external assessments, whereas 1 and 3 involve an internal assessment. Which ones are you comfortable breaking, if any, and does it matter?

Senior leaders in schools are always being scrutinised, and the values and principles they exhibit will be the key indicators of their success or failure. Integrity is one of the most important principles that a senior leader needs to possess and constantly exhibit.

THEY ARE JUST LIKE US

At a recent conference, Estelle Morris shared the aphorism that I paraphrase below:

> The good thing about leaders is that they are just like us. The bad thing about leaders is that they are just like us!

This captures succinctly the idea that there is no wonderful potion that transforms someone into a school leader. Like all endeavours, leadership takes time, effort, commitment and a constant refresh of training and knowledge. A school leader must be truly prepared to re-learn previous habits, understand and be comfortable with the fact that others around them will know more about a particular topic than they do, and live and

---

25   Marc Le Menestrel, INSEAD. Available at: https://images.slideplayer.com/23/6872233/slides/slide_21.jpg

feel the biorhythms of the school calendar. Dealing with ambiguity and being flexible are two other key traits in a school leader.

TRUST

A senior leader must be able to build and sustain trust. In some cultures, trust is loaned. It may be a short-term loan if the leader loses trust through their actions, or a long-term loan that essentially becomes part of the leader's DNA. In both cases, trust is not a permanent feature but is being assessed by everyone constantly. Trust in a leader belongs to those whom a leader leads.

Many authors have discussed the alignment of one's values with one's actions. At a recent Heads' Conference (HMC) in the UK, Steve Mundy used the discordance between United Airlines' tagline of 'Fly the friendly skies' and their actions. In April 2017, four fee-paying passengers were chosen to be involuntarily deplaned; this made the international news and United Airlines later apologised. This illustrates the importance of getting alignment right and the consequence of getting it wrong.

The above message also highlights that a leader's values must be reasonably aligned with the core values of the school. This is particularly true in some countries where one may be asked to do things or (not) say things that are insensitive to the culture. A more direct juxtaposition may be a school whose vision is to create empathetic and compassionate global citizens in a host country in which the human rights record may be challenging. These tensions should be resolved before taking up an international school leadership position.

OUTWARD FACING, INWARD LOOKING

An outward demeanour of calm assurance, verging on hysterical optimism, is an important attribute that all school leaders must possess, whether as an international school leader or someone who leads in the country which they call home. From the minute a senior leader is seen travelling to school to the final email that is sent at night, the tone of interactions says more than the content. The smile, the frown, the cold shoulder, the rush to a meeting, the caught-in-thought interactions that leave a teacher feeling ignored; all these create a culture that gradually threads its way to all people in the school. And that thread could be made of gold or rayon, a simple choice that is universally understood.

While maintaining a positive outward persona, the leader should have a turmoil of doubt about upcoming decisions. The self-reflection, questioning and discussions with others should be constant. Is practice aligned to strategy? Does it fit in a larger discussion? Is this a decision for the students or staff? One decision that is not thought through will likely reverberate around the community, and occasionally lead to a decision needing to be retracted. Too many retractions and all credibility is lost.

LEADERSHIP PRACTICES

There are many theories and practices on leadership. A central tenet to all leadership practices is that leaders must engage themselves and their colleagues with a sense of purpose. Leaders must stay connected to this purpose and be tethered to their feelings. Some key practices for an international school leader include:

- Vision – setting a clear vision for the school, in the context of the host country, and being able to provide the leadership and management skills to enact the strategic direction within agreed timelines.

- Communication – being able to communicate strategically and support the communication of others is one of the most important attributes of a school leader. Good communication fuels success, while poor communication or a lack of communication invariably causes problems. The importance of communicating with diverse groups is always challenging.

- Cultural literacy – as discussed throughout this book, the ability to understand cultural nuances in the international context will enable the head to be empathetic and build capacity within the whole community.

- Team building – being able to create teams who are focused, energetic and able to make successful decisions will not only build trust, but also allow the head to take an overview, dedicate more time to strategic thinking and develop others for senior leadership roles. Section Two contains a diagnostic tool for assessing a team's cohesiveness.

ASIDE

While the performative element of diversity, equity and inclusion practices is secondary to the moral imperative, it cannot be ignored. McKinsey and Co.[26] reports that:

> the business case [for diversity] remains robust but also that the relationship between diversity on executive teams and the likelihood of financial outperformance has strengthened over time.

When creating teams and hiring staff, an international school leader would be wise to take heed of McKinsey's findings. The added dimension of varying cultural groups within an international school means team compositions require careful selection.

Is there a limit to the divergence in thinking that a team can manage? Does the success in the degree of team divergence lie with the team leader or the team as a whole? How can the dissonance that may emerge from the diversity of principles and beliefs of team members be managed so that the decision-making process is not compromised?

And finally, following Sandberg's comment, how many changes that you have introduced will last beyond your tenure? More than ten? Between five and nine? Fewer than five?

---

26 Dixon-Fyle, S. *et al.* (2020) 'Diversity wins: How inclusion matters'. McKinsey & Company. Available at: https://www.mckinsey.com/featured-insights/diversity-and-inclusion/diversity-wins-how-inclusion-matters

MONKEYS

I really do think that any deep crisis is an opportunity to make your life extraordinary in some way.

Martha Beck

Most leaders will recall the figurative expression of a 'monkey on my back', in reference to someone else's problem that has been passed to you. However, international school leaders who have led schools in countries with jungles will invariably have a colourful story or two to tell about actual monkeys. How many schools have a monkey policy for physical or metaphorical monkeys?

One head discusses how they had asked the national wildlife organisation of the country in which they lived to help with some monkeys that kept walking around their lush, green campus. Consequently, the relevant government authority placed a large open container inside the trees that were located on the campus. The idea was that monkeys would drop down into the container to fetch the fruit that had been left there for this purpose. The sides of the container were designed so that the monkeys could not climb out and escape, and were therefore captured and subsequently relocated back to the jungle, far away from the school.

Unfortunately, someone left open the small door on the bottom of the container and a large boa constrictor was later found in the cage with a lump in its length, unable to escape through the door. Not the desired outcome, but when schools are in such close proximity to nature, the intended consequences are rarely the end result. Not only did this mean the head still had to deal with the monkeys, but they also couldn't help thinking of all the large snakes likely to be hiding, just out of sight.

CHANGE LEADERSHIP

The above story is a good metaphor for the care required with change initiatives in international schools. Many international schools enjoy, or put up with, a regular turnover of staff. If key staff or too many staff are being replaced at frequent intervals, then change initiatives need to be planned carefully and implemented cautiously.

There are many theories and much research about change management, but it is a cautionary note for international school leaders to understand this additional factor of frequent staff turnover when implementing school improvements. Otherwise, gates may be left open and one may end up with a constricted process that needs to be abandoned or significantly adapted.

MANAGING IN CRISES

An international school leader should expect to deal with a plethora of incidents that are unlikely to happen in their home country.

One head recounts how they had to charter a Boeing 747 to evacuate their staff during the Arab Spring. Another head recalls watching cruise missiles as they made their way overhead to an, as yet, unknown target.

What do you tell the students and staff in this situation? What sort of risk assessment is done to determine whether school should continue in person or operate online? At what point would you evacuate the country? How do you deal with a cobra that basks in the sun just outside a boarding house on a daily basis? Do you have a typhoon policy?

No training or professional development will cover all the scenarios that you are likely to encounter as an international school leader during your wonderful and inspiring sojourn around the world. It is, therefore, imperative that a head is able to manage significant crises, as it is highly unlikely that an international school head would not have to deal with at least one major issue during their career.

Of course, national schools in lots of countries will have procedures and policies that may appear strange to the outsider. In US schools, three-year-old children routinely practise 'shooter' procedures. Sadly, 'lockdown' or 'intruder' procedures have become standard in too many schools, and international schools are no exception. These cultural norms have been transported from the 'home' country and are even included in some inspection standards.

As an international head, one should use local expertise, be able to make perspicacious judgements and not be too scared of the local wildlife.

CULTURAL CRISES

While managing physical events is one thing, and there will be many, it is often the cultural differences that can really cause problems for an international school leader. The tension between a leader's own values and the core values of the host country in which one works may be the most difficult aspect of being an international school leader.

Before making the decision to accept a school leadership position in another country, it is vital that one is able to navigate the cultural nuances and accept that one is a guest in the host country. How the differing values will manifest themselves in the day-to-day operations of the school is unlikely to be apparent straightaway, but any major differences will be very evident. And it is these major differences that one has to be clear about before deciding to lead a school in another country.

In some Middle Eastern countries, for example, no matter how liberal the country appears to be, there are certain boundaries that must not be crossed. While alcohol may be tolerated in a country (and this is not the case in all Middle Eastern countries), the often-accompanying public celebrations and the occasional brush with the local police are not.

A head relates the sad case of a teacher who, having had a few drinks, decided to verbally confront the local police on duty and ended up in jail for a number of months before being released and deported. It is also well known that if one becomes entangled in a dispute with a local, it is likely that the local will win, no matter the rights of the situation.

Another teacher relates how their car, which was stationary and parked, was hit by another driver who verbally admitted fault. However, when the police report was written, in the local language for insurance purposes, it was clearly stated that the owner of the stationary vehicle was at fault!

It is for these situations that the international head should ensure they have the right contacts for the right people; people who can be called upon to assist at the right time. A few phone calls taken early on in a challenging process can often alleviate much more serious consequences later.

Returning to the monkey problem at the beginning of this section, the head recounts how they placed some stuffed, life-sized tigers around the boarding houses and regularly sprayed them with synthetic tiger urine (bought over the internet – who knew?). This kept the monkeys away for a good six months before they realised that the tigers were not moving. When communicating with staff about the new 'animals', the head said that they had 'released tigers' into the jungle near the boarding houses. A concerned staff member immediately voiced their concerns that they felt this was too dangerous; humour does not always cross cultural differences. It is worth remembering this.

ASIDE

Crises are opportunities for the head to demonstrate leadership, so heads should always take these opportunities and never delegate them. Think back to your last major issue or crisis.

- What would you have done differently?
- Did you write down any learnings or update any policies because of it?
- Was the 'correct' outcome eventually reached, despite a convoluted or poor process?

A crisis situation normally requires a calm and focused response. However, there will invariably be many feelings that emerge.

- How did you manage your emotions?
- How did you manage the emotions of the team or wider community?
- What emotional support did you provide to others?

The five points below from Forbes[27] are succinct and to the point on how to handle a crisis.

1. Move fast.
2. Take responsibility.
3. Be human.
4. Set up channels of communication.
5. Create a plan for next time.

---

27 Kytainyk, V. (28 March 2023) 'How to manage a team and company in a crisis situation'. Forbes. Available at: https://www.forbes.com/sites/forbesbusinesscouncil/2023/03/28/how-to-manage-a-team-and-company-in-a-crisis-situation/?sh=37f8fa6d1f83

NETWORKS

The way a team plays as a whole determines its success. You may have the greatest bunch of individual stars in the world, but if they don't play together, the club won't be worth a dime.

Babe Ruth

Networks are important lifelines to international school leaders. Being a head can be a lonely experience, but being an international head has the potential to be even more isolating.

This is why professional networks are critically important. They provide a touchstone of current educational practices that allows the international leader to compare their own practices and ideas with those in other international schools. Attending relevant international leaders' conferences helps establish collegiate friendships and networks that can be used throughout the year for a myriad of reasons: from checking on prospective teachers' references to sharing thoughts about a new initiative or a difficult situation. These relationships provide a normalising focus for the demanding work of international school leadership.

Most regions in the world have their own professional organisation providing structured opportunities for international staff and students to develop and thrive. Most of the organisations below have similarities in their histories and similar aims, so it is likely that school leaders who travel the world will be able to move relatively easily from one geographical organisation to another.

Below are some of the common UK-focused professional organisations, listed alphabetically. The information has been extracted, and adapted slightly, from the relevant website. All of these organisations hold an annual leaders' conference; many international school leaders will attend more than one conference a year, with some heads seemingly on a 'never-ending tour'. All the information given below is from the respective organisations' websites and was correct at the time of writing.

ASSOCIATION OF BRITISH SCHOOLS OVERSEAS (AoBSO)

Operating under a board, AoBSO strives to connect the best in educational thinking and practices in schools worldwide. AoBSO is a relatively new organisation that was founded following the introduction of the British Schools Overseas (BSO) inspection scheme in 2012.

AoBSO exists to provide BSO schools with a strong, effective global network, recognised by the UK Department for Education, within which best pedagogical and leadership practice is shared in order to achieve and maintain the highest educational outcomes for every student.

To be a member of AoBSO, the school must have undergone a UK DfE BSO accreditation within the last 4 years.

An important principle regarding AoBSO is that it does not intend to duplicate or replace the excellent work of DfE-recognised overseas bodies: BSME, COBIS, FOBISIA and NABSS. AoBSO aims to complement the offers of regional associations and to work in partnership with them to the benefit of all British international schools.

BRITISH SCHOOLS IN THE MIDDLE EAST (BSME)

BSME, founded in 1982, supports a network of high-quality British international schools in the region. In addition, it facilitates an invaluable partnership between member schools and business partners specialising in educational services, products and tools.

BSME offers a robust and varied professional learning calendar to support career progression pathways at all levels, as well as providing high-level sporting, academic and performing arts events for students. Its Headship Induction Partner Programme provides new principals and heads with the support they need while they find their feet in the region. It supports the accreditation of member schools and lobbies regulatory bodies to the benefit of our schools.

COUNCIL OF BRITISH INTERNATIONAL SCHOOLS (COBIS)

COBIS started life in 1986 as COBISEC, a regional organisation for schools in Europe, before it morphed in 2008 into COBIS, a membership association that represents 266 schools globally. High-quality COBIS schools, which educate over 165,000 students and employ more than 17,000 teachers, can be found in more than 80 countries across Europe, Asia, Africa, the Middle East and the Americas. COBIS supporting associates provide a wide range of services and resources to the international schools sector.

Some of the activities in which COBIS is active include:

- Representing members and their interests, lobbying on their behalf with government, education authorities and educational associations.
- Providing quality assurance of the highest standard with their Patron's Accreditation and Compliance.
- Providing opportunities for career advancement through professional learning courses.
- Facilitating valuable networking opportunities, both online and face-to-face, for members based all around the world.
- Hosting engaging, educational and inspiring inter-school competitions and events for students of all ages.
- Providing valuable resources to promote and maintain excellent child protection and safer recruitment standards at member schools, by processing prohibition order checks, providing safeguarding policies and templates, and via partnership with ACRO on the International Certificate for Child Protection.

FEDERATION OF BRITISH INTERNATIONAL SCHOOLS IN ASIA (FOBISIA)

FOBISIA can trace its origins back to 1988, around the same time as COBIS, when some like-minded heads started to meet on an annual basis. It became a formal federation in 2002, initially known as the Federation of British International Schools in South East Asia (FOBISSEA). As more schools joined the federation, it changed its geographical marker and now embraces schools throughout Asia.

FOBISIA supports and promotes high-quality, British-style international education throughout Asia, delivering value for its members through shared professional development, student enrichment and mutual support between member schools in the region.

FOBISIA currently comprises 94 schools in 19 countries spread from Japan to Kazakhstan, Mongolia to Indonesia.

THE HEADS' CONFERENCE (HMC) – INTERNATIONAL

Founded in 1869, HMC was the world's first association for headteachers and currently consists of over 300 members in the British Isles – educating more than 270,000 students – and around 50 further international members across the globe. Needless to say, it is only recently that international schools have joined HMC in any notable numbers.

The association's aims are to serve and support members, to represent their views and to exemplify excellence in education. In particular, HMC seeks to:

- help members and their schools grow and develop
- promote and protect the independence of HMC schools
- encourage and share innovation in HMC schools and more widely
- promote the discussion of national and international educational issues
- inform policy and public opinion with regard to the independent sector.

INDEPENDENT ASSOCIATION OF PREPARATORY SCHOOLS (IAPS)

Founded in 1892 in the UK, IAPS is a professional association for heads with over 660 members in prep, junior and pre-prep schools in the UK and overseas. Schools must meet criteria on teaching a broad curriculum, maintaining excellent standards of pastoral care and keeping staff members' professional development training up to date.

The benefits of IAPS membership include:

- personal, professional support from a team of dedicated advisers

- professional development, with an extensive range of courses designed specifically for prep school staff at all levels
- up-to-date information and bulletins on the latest legal/DfE, and other, guidance; the dedicated members' area of the website contains news, policy examples, specialist resources and advice
- a professional network with prep schools across the globe
- a kitemark of quality for your school to demonstrate that you provide the highest standards of education
- access to a wide range of sporting tournaments and competitions
- a coaching scheme for heads new to IAPS.

LATIN AMERICAN HEADS CONFERENCE (LAHC)

The mission of the LAHC is to bring together centres of educational excellence in South and Central America, reflecting the best of British and international educational practice, in order to share expertise for school improvement in a spirit of reciprocal altruism that benefits all parties.

The association caters specifically for schools which give special importance to the English language, both as a medium for communication and as a language of teaching and learning. Currently, LAHC serves 49 schools in 12 countries.

The LAHC aims to:

- create, develop and nurture a professional learning community within the region by sharing expertise and experience within and beyond the association
- foster cooperation and dialogue among the member schools
- provide mechanisms for context-sensitive school evaluation
- keep member schools informed with respect to developments in educational theory and practice and in particular the areas of bilingual and bicultural education
- encourage and maintain dialogue with relevant educational institutions and associations in Britain and the rest of the world.

THE NATIONAL ASSOCIATION OF BRITISH SCHOOLS IN SPAIN (NABSS)

NABSS was founded in 1978 by a group of leading British schools in Spain. Membership has grown steadily since then, corresponding to the sustained growth of British education within Spain. The association now comprises almost 80 schools who, collectively, are educating more than 45,000 children.

All NABSS-member schools are fully authorised and recognised by the corresponding education authorities in Spain as foreign schools teaching the British education system. In order to obtain this authorisation, they have to be certified by the British Council in Spain after having successfully passed inspections meeting British education standards.

In order to be eligible for NABSS membership, schools must also be well established with a proven track record. New schools that are still developing are not immediately admitted as members.

The main purpose of NABSS is to represent the common interests of these British schools in Spain and to encourage collaboration between them. This extends to providing opportunities for professional development and to keeping schools fully up to date with developments in education in the UK.

ASIDE

Strategic networking or guilty socialising? The purpose of the interactions will determine whether it is strategic for the good of the school or socialising for personal gain. The organisations above will provide a rich and diverse range of opportunities for the international school leader to become known, consolidate their standing or provide counsel, depending on where they are at in their careers. Creating an extended team may not seem important or pressing, but being able to call upon individuals for advice or support is invaluable.

Some heads will attend four or even five conferences a year; others might be more judicious in their conference visits. Regardless of the number that a head attends, how many heads attend conferences with particular networking goals in mind and review these goals at the end of the conference?

ONLINE

If you don't get out there and define yourself, you'll be quickly and inaccurately defined by others.

Michelle Obama

The word 'online' brings most teachers out in a sweat as they recall the days of the COVID pandemic, where teachers had to manage both synchronous and asynchronous teaching using their laptop or other device. While this period in history wrought so much pain, suffering and loss, there was some positivity that emerged.

Teachers demonstrated resilience and the ability to adapt quickly to change. Before the pandemic, most changes that took place in schools happened at glacial speed. Some factors that contribute to this slow progress include:

- the lack of time to devote to change when there is so much involved in preparing and facilitating good lessons
- needing to keep on top of the mandated administration
- the fact that the natural rhythm of change in schools revolves around the annual cycle of renewal
- the nature of the staff involved in the profession; people enjoy teaching for a variety of reasons, one being the security in routines that is disturbed when change occurs.

During the COVID pandemic, leaders had to make many decisions in a short space of time. A head recalls the decision they had to make about whether to allow teachers to teach from home, their home being in another country. Noting that the country of the school was in a strict lockdown while the home country of some staff members was not, and with staff wellbeing a central concern during that period, the decision was made to allow staff to travel back to their home country with various parameters firmly stipulated. When parents found out that some teachers were teaching from their home country, however, the issue exploded and was escalated to the board. This resentment was felt particularly strongly by those parents who could not return home, whether because they were local, as a result of their work commitments or because their home country was in lockdown. Regardless of the reason, the strength of negative feeling associated with this decision was surprising but clearly exacerbated by the personal circumstances of the parents.

PROFESSIONAL LEARNING

One of the most exciting developments emerging from the pandemic is that people now understand they can communicate and learn online. It might not always be as comfortable, accurate or efficient as face-to-face communication, but it is far better to meet online than not meet at all. It is also highly effective in terms of time and cost.

This presents a great opportunity for schools to develop their own professional learning programme for their staff using people all over the world. One head discusses that they are in the third year of an online professional learning programme that has involved Tom Sherrington, Roy Blatchford, Jackie Beare and the magician Joshua Jay, among over 40 other presenters.

The topics that have been covered range from generative AI to cognitive load theory in action to public speaking. The international school leader has an amazing opportunity to develop the best up-to-date and relevant learning for staff at a fraction of the normal cost.

TRANSPARENT COMMUNICATION

As we have seen from politicians, there is much to celebrate in communicating directly and quickly with the relevant community. There is a range of online tools a senior leader can use to connect with their community: from blogs to Twitter (currently known as X) to Instagram to LinkedIn. The latter three offer a quick and easy way to promote student or school achievements. Not every country uses X or Instagram equally, and this should be noted when developing a communication strategy with an international company. A blog takes more time but gives the head a platform to espouse their philosophies, beliefs and thinking about education and all related matters.

In today's social media arena, a school needs to carve out its position, and the head has a responsibility to shape the message and image of the school; to own the brand. As Michelle Obama writes, if you don't do it, someone else will fill the void with their own agenda.

One head commented that they used an international company to develop their website, which had embedded Twitter feeds. They believed that they would be able to change these later to Instagram posts, but learned that this was not an easy fix!

ONLINE HATE

Sadly, in the current climate, anonymous, vicious online attacks are becoming more prevalent against both teachers and students. As anonymous individuals feel untouchable and a lack of respect becomes normalised, schools should follow established procedures to deal with hate messages.

Different countries have widely different reporting mechanisms and laws when it comes to online abuse. Given the prevalence of such abuse, the international school leader should establish clear processes and policies. These will need to be relevant to their particular country, as they will vary significantly from country to country. An overview of a simple process might be:

1. Keep the evidence secure. The nature of the attack will determine how the evidence should be stored.

2. Report the abuse to the relevant platform using their reporting procedures.

3. Seek advice and support from external agencies. These may be able to help you determine whether a local law has been broken. The Crown Prosecution Service (CPS) based in the UK is one platform that may be a source of information and advice.

4. Inform the police if necessary.

The following summary is from the CPS.[28] UK law recognises five types of hate crime on the basis of: race, religion, disability, sexual orientation and transgender identity. Any crime in the UK can be prosecuted as a hate crime if the offender has either:

- demonstrated hostility based on race, religion, disability, sexual orientation or transgender identity

or

- been motivated by hostility based on race, religion, disability, sexual orientation or transgender identity.

While laws in different countries will vary widely, the important thing is to communicate a zero tolerance policy to online abuse to all stakeholders, have procedures in place for when it does happen and know the reporting processes of the country. Again, having a direct line to someone in the cyber crimes unit would be useful for an international school leader.

DATA PROTECTION

The European Union General Data Protection Regulation (GDPR) came into effect in May 2018. It governs how personal data of individuals may be processed and transferred. An international school hiring teachers from the EU is subject to the law. Furthermore, countries have their own data privacy laws that might resemble the GDPR and so these would need to be adhered to in conjunction with other countries' laws.

The GDPR requires organisations to have a data protection officer. It would serve the international school head well to follow these procedures, if they do not already, as it is likely that some staff will be hired from an EU country and, as staff become far more data savvy, there will be more and more demands made of schools.

Article 46 of the GDPR essentially states that data can only be transferred to a third party outside the EU if that third party has appropriate data

---

28 'Hate crime', Crown Prosecution Service. © Crown Copyright, 2023. Available at: https://www.cps.gov.uk/crime-info/hate-crime

control mechanisms in place.[29] This may not be strictly adhered to at the present time, but will likely become increasingly relevant as data is commodified in ways that we do not yet know. The very basic needs for a school are to have a data officer/controller, a policy in place that adheres to local privacy laws as well as GDPR (if staff are recruited from the EU), regular training for staff about the capture and use of data, and a sensible approach that adheres to data laws while managing the operations of the school. It is too easy for this to slip into another process for the 'policy police,' something to be avoided at all costs.

CYBER ATTACKS

There has been an uptick in the number of cyber attacks on organisations, and schools are not exempted from this debilitating crime. If a school does fall victim to these malicious acts, a plan is going to be required quickly; the complexity of the plan will depend on the depth of the attack. Given the connectivity we now use, it is likely that an attack will hit the much wider infrastructure and potentially infect and halt all computer activity in the school.

One school that did fall victim to such an attack was without computing capabilities for four days. The first action was to identify and isolate the threat, which came from a ransomware virus called Sodinokibi. Having isolated the virus, the school then rebuilt the platform and infrastructure with help from a company based in the UK. Thankfully, the Google data was unharmed, but the rest of the data was corrupted and unsalvageable. Once restored, the system was tested thoroughly and the weakness in the system where the virus penetrated was secured. A full report was prepared, again using external expertise, and a training programme for all staff established.

It was fortunate that the school used Google as this meant that the work of teachers and students was safe. One of the precautions the school now has is to back up all their Google data, just in case Google is hacked! The school now has regular external penetration testing and a robust process for staff training that includes sending out phishing emails to staff, who

---

29   General Data Protection Regulation, article 46. Available at: https://gdpr-info.eu/art-46-gdpr/

must attend ongoing cyber security training, in the same way that they attend safeguarding training.

ASIDE

Schools cannot function without using technology and being online. As a result, a large proportion of schools' capital expenditure is utilised on hardware. But how much effort and finances are directed at keeping the computer systems secure?

How would you rate your school against the following?

Description	Fully aligned	In progress	Not started
Adherence to the host country's personal data protection law and GDPR if applicable. This might include: policy management, processing individuals' data, information security, third-party risks and training awareness.			
The curriculum incorporates the internet of things, augmented and virtual reality learning, makerspaces, robotics and coding for all students.			
Artificial intelligence chatbots are used to automatically mark long-answer examination questions, as well as using other adaptive digital learning environments.			
Termly penetration testing of the network and related systems, undertaken by an external company.			
Regular differentiated training of staff for phishing and similar threats using an external organisation.			
Regular use of internet tools to 'guess' staff passwords, and informing staff that they must change their password.			
Two-factor authentication for all access to any computer network managed by the school.			

PURPOSE

Champions keep playing until they get it right.

Billie Jean King

With the globalisation of the economy, international schools are ideally placed to educate people for a better future. Reports from organisations like the OECD and UNICEF articulate the educational needs and desires of western societies for the future.

Given that we aim to educate people to be better at governing the world than the current generation, a school curriculum will require elements beyond the usual siloed, subject-based requirements. The mission of many international schools is to educate *everyone* because schools are communities. International schools, in particular, become the central focus for so many people.

Our purposeful and accidental interconnectedness with all forms of life on Earth have been growing and growing but are now so prevalent that we cannot ignore the wrecking ball that we have hurled at the world. We must educate young people explicitly about our negative impact while managing to convey the amazing accomplishments of so many people and organisations.

And all this we do must be for the good of all humankind, emanating compassion and demonstrating forethought that we readily talk about yet find difficult to achieve. This is further compounded in international schools where there is a recognisable cultural distinction between parent groups. However, through careful planning and helpful measures, a leader can make a good attempt at the Gordian knot of culture and climate in schools.

The connected thinking in international schools is probably as varied as it is in national schools. Blind adherence to national standards and curricula traps some international schools in their offerings, being more 'British' or 'American' than schools back home, often representing a bygone era through rose-tinted glasses.

Elements of any curriculum should include key snapshots of world history so that students can place our current mess in the bigger mess of world events. It might, surprisingly, give strength to young people worried about the future. An understanding of religious belief systems, a perspective on politics across the world, from (benign) dictatorships to democratic rule, an appreciation of our place in the world and how we place the world in the classroom are all of critical importance as we see greater nationalism, greater fragmentation of societies and increased gaps in wealth.

How people learn best is well documented and the explosion of neuroscience into how we learn in schools has offered great insight for educationalists to remodel curricular and learning opportunities. The Common Ground Collaborative – a global, not-for-profit educational network – refers to schools defining learning principles, an idea that many schools now do although it is very much a concept that did not widely exist 20 years ago.

From the Socratic method and Harkness tables to the didactic traditionalists of many classrooms; from paper and pens to iPads and laptops and back again. The inclusion of research into schools is overwhelming for some, '*initiatitis*' being a common ailment.

DISTILLING TIME

One problem for teachers and school leaders is finding time to think, to discuss and to refine ideas. We are time deficient in most aspects of our lives and this is no different in schools. We sow a scattering of seeds on semi-fertile ground in the hope that one or two will take hold, rather than cultivating a few choice organisms under controlled conditions with a dedicated agriculturalist.

In schools, this might translate to employing a professional researcher who could work with individuals, teams and the whole school, devising strategies that are relevant and focused. Working with teachers to conduct some action research or educating parents about why their child needs an iPad at the age of seven. Bringing the right people together from inside and outside the school, forming partnerships with a local law firm or NGO. These would all fall within the researcher's realm of responsibility. Such appointments have been made in international schools, and the researcher is able to condense, articulate and understand schools in a way that an academic working from a university may not.

A researcher is able to give people one of our greatest gifts – time to think.

LEARNING TO ENGAGE, ENGAGING TO LEARN

Students in early secondary education should be given the opportunity to experience a plethora of learning strategies, including learning with a teacher who is learning the subject at the same time as the students. This would take a confident, intelligent teacher, trusting parents and inquisitive students who are all allowed to participate in the process. As students progress along their educational journey, they should be allowed to accelerate in subjects in which they are confident and take time over those subjects where they require consolidation.

Core learning would be part of the journey and this core would not just be mathematics and English, but politics, religion, economics, world history and the arts. The 'healthy' aspect of the curriculum revolves around the obvious elements of exercise, diet, mental health and wellbeing for the entire community. Involving staff and parents is vital in order to slow down and eventually reverse the worrying trends in young people of obesity, lack of self-esteem and lack of confidence. Much of it, we are told, is rooted in the use of 'anti-social' media. The social aspect of the curriculum is all about learning to engage, engaging to learn.

The UN Sustainable Development Goals provide an ideal framework that can be adopted and adapted by schools to make a real difference in the world. International schools have a responsibility to engage with the local community, to be involved in making a difference in people's lives; not creating posters or PowerPoints about the issues but actually being a part of the solution.

This has been done to great effect in many schools across the world, whether national or international. The British School of Kathmandu responded immediately, on the ground, to the devastating earthquake in Nepal in April 2015. Schools by their nature are caring communities.

Too many people, including too many world leaders, fail to take responsibility for the catastrophic climate changes we are inflicting on our planet and our young people. In a similar vein, teachers and leaders have a collective responsibility to create a climate in schools where everyone can flourish. Ethos, climate, atmosphere are all proxies for how we treat each other and the types of relationships that we champion in schools.

DIGITAL ACCEPTANCE

Overcoming digital ignorance for teachers, school leaders and parents will be an issue for another generation until the digital natives become digital leaders of nations, hopefully beyond the examples of some of our current world leaders, often seen on Twitter (currently known as X).

In the meantime, schools are already incorporating the best young thinking into curricular designs, with students helping, supporting and guiding teachers. Schools have partnerships with Microsoft, Google and Apple and are exploring the use of technology in learning. Universities recognise the power of technology and are creating adaptive gaming environments for school learning.

Schools are submitting examination portfolios in art that utilise virtual reality. Digital ignorance is fast becoming digital wisdom. Every school needs staff members who can stay up to date and drive technology for learning, knowing where to locate both the brake and accelerator, and how to use them effectively.

LAWYERING-UP

Against a backdrop of increasing parental complaints, with more parents lawyering-up far more frequently and staff and parents knowing their rights and, at times, their entitlements, it is not surprising that these relationships are often the most time consuming to manage. In their first term at an international school, one new head received a lawsuit against both the school and them personally for expelling a boy who had caused significant harm to others. Gone are the days of parents being deferential to educators.

As a minimum, an international school head should be covered under the school's Director and Officer insurance. In addition, there should be a clause in their contract that provides indemnity, where the school will cover the full cost associated with *any* legal action directed at the head.

ASIDE

Here are some questions that all international school leaders should be able to answer convincingly.

1.   What is the purpose of education, and how does your international school support this goal?
2.   How do you help students discover their passion in life?
3.   How does the school support the development of students' personal qualities alongside the academic?
4.   How does the school engage meaningfully with the multitude of social issues, both locally and globally?
5.   How should an educated person think and speak about the world?
6.   What action does the school take to support students to rectify the mess that exists in the world?

QUALITY

Rarely are opportunities presented to you in a perfect way. In a nice little box with a yellow bow on top. 'Here, open it, it's perfect. You'll love it.' Opportunities – the good ones – are messy, confusing and hard to recognize. They're risky. They challenge you.

Susan Wojcicki

With professionals potentially coming from across the world with varying educational philosophies and experiences, and turnover in some international schools relatively high, it is vital that international school leaders put in place systems that ensure consistency and quality of instruction.

The school's mission, vision and values are central to how we teach, how we conduct ourselves in a professional capacity, both in and out of school, and how we develop our practice.

The use of professional development portfolios (PDPs) is one tool that some international schools have turned to, in the hope of continuously improving students' learning through the increased efficacy of teachers. It is a differentiated process that allows a high degree of autonomy, with the associated high level of responsibility.

Professional portfolios do not just have to be focused on teachers; they are equally helpful to develop administrative staff. A comprehensive, inclusive framework for the whole school contributes to a positive learning culture.

A PDP provides evidence that supports teachers' and administrative colleagues' professionalism when measured against standards.

Professional learning should be founded on the understanding that development of new beliefs, knowledge, methodology and skills arises organically out of the needs of the students, the teacher and the evolution of the school. Therefore, an ongoing process of recognising and recording contemplative practices provides a more well-rounded, realistic and fuller portrait of teaching and learning than the traditional appraisal model.

It is expected that staff actively engage in the processes of assessing, re-assessing and developing teaching and learning practices, aiming for significant progress in student learning. Improvement of skills comes from deliberate practice. That is, practice that is thoughtful and is directed towards development of expertise, rather than simple repetition of tasks and activities.

The PDP should lead to the sharing and diffusion of an ever-expanding range of good working practices throughout a school, while acknowledging that it is beneficial to students to experience a range of teaching and learning practices during their time in school.

A head has a choice, whether to take the opportunity and be challenged by the intimately messy process of raising standards, or to allow the status quo to persist, perhaps tinkering around the edges; no one else in the school has the authority to make this decision, and no decision is more important. So take the opportunity afforded to you as head, and create a world-beating process for staff professional growth.

TEACHER PORTFOLIOS

The ongoing completion of the PDP is viewed as an essential aspect of a teacher's development, and time should be allocated to it at the start of each term and during planning and preparation time. Each teacher should be expected to maintain their own portfolio of professional development. The upkeep of the portfolio will be an ongoing activity not an end-of-term or end-of-year event to be completed on a teacher's to-do list.

All PDP plans should be reviewed and agreed by the appropriate reviewer. Feedback to teachers from lesson observations should take place within 24 hours and should always be shared. Colleagues should conduct learning walks as part of the ongoing good practice.

The following list of core elements might form part of every teacher's PDP:

- Anonymous feedback from age-appropriate students about a particular/general aspect of learning in your classroom. A selection of questionnaires made available to teachers, although they may wish to submit their own questionnaire to their immediate senior leader for consideration.

- Each teacher discusses with a member of their team areas of pedagogy which they wish to explore and improve. This will be their pedagogical focus.

- Ideally, peer observations should be developed as a triad but, because of timetabling restraints, they may have to take place as a pair. If working in a triad, then two colleagues may observe a third colleague with a specific focus. Feedback is always shared in the triad. In general, teachers choose their triad but there may be instances when a particular pairing or triad is decided by their reviewer.

- Lesson observations or partial-lesson observations by a reviewer, who will be looking for aspects of excellent practice as described in the pedagogical rubric. (See one example of a pedagogical rubric in Section Two.)

- It is not expected that all elements from the pedagogical rubric are met within a single lesson observation. However, it is expected that all elements are met over a period of time. There are four possible outcomes for the individual descriptors within the pedagogical rubric:

  - Instructor – the teacher has mastered this element of the rubric and is able to conduct continuing professional development (CPD) in this area and support colleagues.

  - Confident – the teacher is confident in their own practice of this element but further consolidation is required before they conduct CPD and support colleagues.

  - Not observed – this element has not yet been observed or demonstrated by the teacher.

  - Not yet met – the teacher has tried to demonstrate this element but has not yet met the confident descriptor.

- Evidence of adherence by the teacher to the curriculum, the mission, vision and values of the school and professional standards for teachers are to be fully documented by the teacher.
- Sharing professional learning with colleagues.

And for some staff it might be possible to include the following.

- Whole-school strategic priorities and school action plans should be incorporated into the PDP if applicable.
- Creation of and participation in a professional learning community to explore recent research about pedagogy, neuroscience, cognitive science or other related aspects of education.
- An action research project that is well-defined, measurable, achievable, realistic and timely. This could be prepared for publication in a scholarly journal.
- A literature review of an educational topic that is shared with colleagues or prepared for publication in a scholarly journal.

PROFESSIONAL IMPROVEMENT PLANS

When a staff member has insufficient evidence in their portfolio, or if there is another reason why the staff member does not meet the required standard as outlined in the expectations section, then a tightly focused and time-sensitive professional improvement plan (PIP) or similar should be utilised.

Insufficient evidence could result from a staff member not engaging fully with their PDP responsibilities, having difficulty in meeting the standards in the pedagogical rubric or consistently failing an aspect of the standards for teachers.

In this situation, a member of the senior leadership team will meet with the staff member and agree a strategy to rectify the issue(s).

- It is vital that problems are addressed as soon as possible.
- It is anticipated that almost all problems will be solved, on a day-to-day basis, by the staff member's reviewer and that very little intervention from a senior leader will be required.

- On encountering a problem in a staff member's performance, a reviewer must decide whether the problem is minor or major. In the case of minor problems, it is expected that the reviewer will attempt to find a solution without informing a senior leader.

- The reviewer should approach the appropriate senior leader at the point when they feel that they cannot solve the problem or that it is a major issue rather than a minor one.

- The senior leader and reviewer will attempt to resolve the situation through a variety of means, including the possible use of the PIP.

- If the senior leader considers that a problem could lead to any doubt as to whether the teacher's contract should be renewed or could lead to a disciplinary action or termination of service before completion of the staff member's contract, then they should immediately inform the appropriate phase leader, who must in turn inform the head.

It is important that minor problems are dealt with promptly and with a minimum of formality. Such problems are generally due to a lack of understanding, poor communication or insufficient clarity; an informal discussion will address most concerns of this type.

In the case of more major or repeated minor problems, it must be clearly and explicitly explained to the staff member that their performance is below the minimum expected standards in a specified area or areas and that these shortcomings must be addressed. At this point the reviewer should inform the appropriate senior leader, but will retain control of the situation, unless the senior leader considers that they should step in. If the senior leader considers that they should not step in, then a personal improvement plan (PIP) will be initiated, designed to address the shortfall in performance.

As a general rule, it should be noted that reviewers – especially in relation to direct teaching duties – are expected to discover shortcomings and deal with them before they reach a level of concern that requires the reviewer to hand over the situation to a senior leader. This is one more reason why reviewers must assiduously use learning walks and other methods of monitoring teaching and learning.

There will be occasions on which a serious shortfall becomes apparent with no prior indications. Any such occasion must be immediately reported to the relevant executive leader.

ASIDE

Quality assurance or quality control? Obviously, both are important and, in the context of education, schools have no end of guidelines and procedures to provide a laser-sharp focus on quality. In the UK, the quality of education is measured by Ofsted against intent, implementation and impact. The first two are concerned with quality assurance, while impact is about the outcome; this is the quality control aspect of education and, when done correctly, provides feedback for recursive improvement.

Lesson observations are the obvious mechanism for quality control in schools, but learner outcomes should be viewed through many lenses, including students' personal characteristics. Ofsted references the 'behaviour and attitudes' of students but does not really get to grips with the intricacies and richness of these. It very much feels as if they are stuck in 19th-century expectations of students.

How long will it be until governments place a greater emphasis on the personal characteristics, the attributes and values that schools help shape? Until such a time, schools will continue to graduate some students who are disingenuous, discordant and disengaged young people, who care little for others.

- Do your quality assurance and control procedures take into account staff turnover?
- How differentiated are your quality assurance processes?
- Do your procedures really trust staff or are they designed to catch people out?
- Do staff receive comments about their professionalism (see chapter on Expectations), as opposed to their teaching?

REMUNERATION

An investment in knowledge always pays the best interest.

Benjamin Franklin

Remuneration is a serious consideration for all staff, including the head, when choosing to work at an international school. Even in schools where the head has delegated authority over the budget, there is very little room to manoeuvre when it comes to salaries because the salary and benefits package forms such a large proportion of a school's operational budget, certainly in most day schools.

Ensuring salary levels and associated benefits are competitive will increase the likelihood of attracting quality teachers and associate staff to the school, and of these staff remaining at the school for an extended period of time. In some cases, the head does not have any discretion when it comes to staff salaries. This is often the case if the school has a single owner or is part of a for-profit group.

MORAL IMPERATIVE

In cases where the head does have a degree of autonomy over the salary structure, and there are clear inequalities between staff salaries, there is an imperative to begin to address these inequalities. In some regions of the world, senior leaders may find that their local staff and/or 'migrant' workers are paid a paltry monthly salary.

In such cases, various ways to increase packages have been adopted by some schools. The obvious is differential salary increases. In some instances, it may be possible to increase the salaries of the lowest-paid workers by as much as, say, 30% without it having a significant impact on the operational budget of the school. This reflects the gross inequalities that exist and that some people are prepared to sustain.

An annual bonus is another way to support lower-paid staff. Monetary collections from better-paid staff for special celebrations and outings, while very well intended, maintain an increasing divide between staff, institutionalise the financial discrepancies and essentially let the school off the hook.

Local or 'migrant' workers ensure the smooth operation of the schools they love, and often work long hours, sometimes late into the night. Without such a dedicated, loyal and committed group of workers, many of the most successful international schools in the world would not function smoothly, particularly in places where local labour is cheap.

One of the biggest moral imperatives on an international school head is to address this pay discrimination.

EXPAT EXPECTATIONS

The 'expat' teacher, as opposed to the 'migrant' worker, expects a good level of remuneration. The following have become the norm in many international schools: a competitive salary, housing provided or an allowance (although neither of these benefits is normally offered for schools in Europe), flights and medical insurance for self and family, school places for at least two dependent children and an end-of-contract gratuity.

The local foreign teacher, often the partner of someone who is already in the country or is moving to the country because of their partner's work, often receives a salary that is lower than their 'expat' colleagues, despite doing the same work.

Since the 1980s, when international schools began to appear in larger numbers and before the current proliferation of international schools, the salary structures that emerged led to discrimination against the local foreign teacher who was already living in the country. Invariably this local foreign teacher was female, and this discriminatory practice became embedded and normalised in some international schools.

Many schools have already changed, or are in the process of changing, this practice. In countries with strong regulatory bodies where regulations are enforced, this practice would not have been allowed; indeed it is illegal in some countries. Not only is it the right thing for a head to do, to equalise salaries, but it also alleviates many simmering issues and helps create a more collegiate culture.

The benefits part of an 'expat' teacher's package does not usually 'double up'. For example, if an 'expat' teaching couple is employed, then annual flights may be provided for both of them but each individually does not get their own flight and a flight for their partner, as this would, in effect, mean they would receive four flights for two people. The same argument is extended to the local foreign teacher if their partner receives benefits from their place of work, although care must be taken when the external partner of a foreign teacher loses benefits.

INTERNATIONAL HEADS' REMUNERATION

Remuneration for heads varies significantly by nationality, location, school, experience, gender and a whole host of other factors. One consultant states that American international school leaders are generally paid higher and have better packages than their British counterparts, partly, he believes, because 'Brits' are uncomfortable when discussing money and themselves so there is a double barrier to overcome. This is worth bearing in mind when negotiating your package.

Heads should remember that they are solely responsible for negotiating their own salary and benefits; there is no international regulatory framework or standard that is adhered to by governing bodies, owners or management groups. It is also worth noting that local laws shape the parameters of what can and cannot be offered by schools.

In some schools, a governing body consisting solely of parents or a chair of governors who is a parent may be less inclined to provide the competitive salary that a head may expect. Whereas if the chair works as a CEO for a large organisation, they may have a more favourable perspective on the head's salary and benefits package.

Much like the 'expat' teacher, there are standard expectations among heads when it comes to their own remuneration: basic salary, housing or a housing allowance (if outside of Europe), flights (possibly business class), medical insurance for self and family and at least two free school places for dependent children.

However, there are far more additional options to consider: tuition for university/college-aged dependents, life insurance for self and partner, annual bonus linked to key performance indicators, car and driver with all expenses paid, in-house assistance for cleaning, cooking and child support, membership of a local social/sports club, paid flights and hotel for partner to attend conferences, digital package (mobile phone and laptop as a minimum), paid sabbatical after, say, seven years of service, final gratuity payment on completion of service, employment for partner, tax advice from one of the big four ... the list of possibilities can be endless.

It is unlikely that an international head will be given all these benefits, and one would argue that they should not ask for all of them. However, it is worth noting that some schools are able to tailor their package to the particular needs of the head at the time of appointment or salary review, especially if the head has solid experience from reputable international schools and is reasonable in their own expectations.

In countries where income tax is paid, the head should note that benefits-in-kind are often taxable and these can reduce the head's basic salary significantly; business class flights can quickly lose their lustre. In these instances, a wise head would consult a local tax adviser during the negotiations and maybe negotiate a payment at the end of the contract, when the head leaves the country, that is essentially tax-free.

The same consultant who offered his observations about the difference between Americans and 'Brits' uses the rule-of-thumb measure that a head should receive approximately twice that of the highest paid senior leader in the school, who in turn should receive approximately twice that of the highest paid teacher in the school. Of course, these are all arbitrary figures, but they provide a modicum of detail for international leaders around the world.

Heads should be reasonable in their expectations and negotiations, while making sure they do not accept a package they will quickly resent.

Remember, too, to include a clause in the contract that provides for a regular review of salary and package.

PENSIONS

With all these benefits it is easy to overlook pension provision, particularly if the school leader or 'expat' teacher is relatively young. This has likely been 'missed' by many international schools and may only be provided if the local laws stipulate such a provision. In these cases, it is unlikely that the pension provision would represent a significant contribution to the head's final pension unless one stays in the country for a significant amount of time.

Therefore, it is all the more important that school leaders plan early and carefully about life after work; as one moves enthusiastically between countries and continents, time passes quickly and retirement, all too soon, becomes a stark reality. Some countries have strict laws about retirement age that need to be carefully checked prior to accepting employment.

There is a forest of wealth management consultants who target international schools and their staff with investment opportunities and pension schemes. A highly cautious approach is probably too reckless when dealing with some of these weasels.

ASIDE

How do you go about negotiating your package? Here are some pointers to think about.

1. Know the market trends. Use your network to find out the salaries of other heads in a similar position in a similar region of the world.

2. Understand the taxation requirements of the country you are about to work in and whether there is a reciprocal tax agreement with your home country. Pay particular attention to taxation of benefits-in-kind. Business class flights might be appealing, but they lose their appeal if you have to pay tax on them.

3. Always be honest in your interactions; never lie. This doesn't mean that you overshare.

4. Decide how best to prioritise and frame your requirements. Most schools will ask about the head's current package.

5. Ensure everything agreed is written into the contract.

SAFEGUARDING

Children are the world's most valuable resource and its best hope for the future.

John F. Kennedy

Horrific stories of child sexual abuse rightly make international headlines, and these headlines include incidents in national and international schools.

Thankfully, safeguarding procedures are now well embedded into most schools. It is of critical importance when it comes to international schools, where teachers and leaders move around the world through various jurisdictions, some tighter than others, that the school's procedures are robust and regularly reviewed.

The NSPCC[30] writes that safeguarding is:

- protecting children from abuse and maltreatment
- preventing harm to children's health or development
- ensuring children grow up with the provision of safe and effective care
- taking action to enable all children and young people to have the best outcomes.

Child protection is part of safeguarding and is about protecting children who are suffering, or are suspected of suffering, ill treatment.

---

30 NSPCC. Available at: https://learning.nspcc.org.uk/safeguarding-child-protection/getting-started-safeguarding-child-protection

There is a wealth of literature on safeguarding and child protection. This section aims to provide a very, very brief overview and signpost other sources for information.

GUARDING THE DOOR

The first step for international schools is to ensure the best possible practices are followed when hiring staff. No head wants to be responsible for hiring someone who has a history of mistreating children. A minimum requirement for most schools when hiring someone would be:

- three references, including one from the current head of the most recent school
- a phone conversion with the head or senior leader at the most recent school(s)
- a social media check
- an identity check
- a qualifications check
- questions on safeguarding at interview
- police checks from the countries in which the applicant has lived and was born
- a check against child sex registries in countries in which the candidate has worked.

The website of the National Protective Security Authority (NPSA)[31] contains details of how to obtain a police check from the countries where a prospective teacher has worked.

The International Task Force on Child Protection (ITFCP) has a thorough document that outlines extensive checks for school recruitment.[32] Having carried out these checks, there must be clear policies in place on what to do when issues arise. For example, what should a head do if a social media check uncovers a series of abusive social media comments

---

31 National Protective Security Authority. Available at: https://www.npsa.gov.uk/employment-screening

32 International Task Force on Child Protection. Available at: https://resources.finalsite.net/images/v1543573914/cis/antsvzqr0yb8aoclkbj9/Recommended-Recruitment-and-Screening-Practices.pdf

that clearly condemn? Would multiple comments be different from an isolated comment? Clearly, the context and language used are relevant. These issues arise far more frequently than first anticipated; a process and system have to be established and adhered to by the school.

A head having conditionally offered a job to a teacher, subject to a satisfactory social media check, had to withdraw the offer when inappropriate and offensive social media comments were found. The teacher tried to downplay the comments but did not understand the local context. In another example, a head reflects that a prospective teacher was asked to remove one political comment but continued to be employed by the school.

SCHOOL PROCESSES

Once staff are employed, they form part of the child protection and safeguarding network within a school. There are many definitions relating to safeguarding but all are based around protecting and preventing harm to children.

A level-based needs assessment of students' welfare and wellbeing, with appropriate secure and confidential software to log, monitor and assess students' ongoing needs, is found in most schools. This allows for a proactive rather than a reactive approach to safeguarding.

Either on a weekly or bi-weekly basis, the designated safeguarding team will meet and review all cases logged by staff members. A separate process will be used for those serious situations that arise where it is not appropriate to wait for the regular triage meeting. The safeguarding team will normally consist of the designated safeguarding lead(s), the deputy safeguarding lead(s), at least one school counsellor, members of the pastoral team and possibly the nurses. They will bring their expertise and historical case knowledge to ascertain the course of action in each individual case.

Schools should also ensure that they have a policy on providing references for staff who are leaving their school. In some instances the school, and possibly the referee providing the reference, may be open to litigation if they provide a reference that is overly positive and omits crucial information, or is too negative or provides no information when there are details to share. In the international school context, it is crucial for schools to provide fair and accurate references as teachers travel the globe and are easily lost in the myriad of different local laws and weak enforcement.

EXTERNAL AGENCIES

One of the most difficult aspects of safeguarding in international schools can be access to external agencies when required. Some agencies may exist but be detrimental to students' wellbeing because of the way in which they work. These assessments by the school of external agencies are normally built up over time in real situations, which is an added factor for the international head to consider.

By definition, a school needs to be proactive, not reactive, in all safeguarding matters. The KCSIE 2023 report[33] from the UK government provides statutory guidance for schools and colleges in England. It details comprehensive guidance that can be utilised for international schools.

The Council of International Schools has an excellent section on its website about child protection and safeguarding.

The International Centre for Missing & Exploited Children (ICMEC) is another very useful and helpful resource for international schools.

EXTERNAL REPORTING

In some countries, it is too easy for international schools not to report serious safeguarding issues that arise, because the process is perhaps deemed too difficult. There should never be an excuse not to report an individual where a thorough investigation has been carried out that led to the termination of employment for that individual.

Of course, there are many scenarios that arise where children need protecting, some of which involve abuse being committed by one or both parents. The latter scenario is one of the most difficult to deal with in international schools if external agencies are of poor quality and government legislation is non-existent. In international schools, cultural differences are frequently posited as reasons for abuse. Schools should

---

33 *Keeping children safe in education.* (2023) DfE. Available at: https://assets.publishing. service.gov.uk/media/64f0a68ea78c5f000dc6f3b2/Keeping_children_safe_in_ education_2023.pdf

never accept this as a legitimate position to uphold. Abuse is abuse. Reference to the school's values and the support of a local staff member, perhaps with a skilled school counsellor, are helpful to begin to address these complex issues.

For UK-registered teachers, reporting serious issues if a teacher has resigned or been dismissed can be done through the teacher regulation agency.[34] If the nature of the serious misconduct involves child sexual abuse, then the school should contact the Disclosure and Barring Service.[35]

The ICMEC[36] has details about reporting child abuse for some other countries.

In cases of serious child abuse, the head should never agree that the abuser should 'leave quietly'. It is the school's responsibility to protect children, no matter how difficult this may prove in an international setting.

ASIDE

Can everyone in the school, from the cleaners to the CEO, answer the questions below?

1. How do you raise a concern you may have about a child's welfare?
2. What are the signs of a child suffering neglect?
3. How has your attitude to child safeguarding evolved over the past five years?
4. What is the difference between safeguarding and child protection?
5. How could a parent stop their child from seeking help?
6. How many school parents are not aware of the school's safeguarding procedures and policies?

---

34 'Report serious teacher misconduct'. Available at: https://www.gov.uk/report-teacher-misconduct
35 'Barring referrals'. Available at: https://www.gov.uk/guidance/barring-referrals
36 International Centre for Missing & Exploited Children. Available at: https://www.icmec.org/education-portal/reporting-mechanisms/

TRUSTEES

Effective school boards act as catalysts for change, guiding the vision and strategy for educational excellence within their communities.

Michael Fullan

International school boards are as varied as the schools they serve. Whether you have a board of trustees or governors, a school council or the school is operated as a business or owned by a benefactor, school leaders need to pay attention to these critical relationships, particularly if the international school operates in a country with loose regulations and little oversight. Even if there are clear regulations, they might not be applied equally to foreign residents as they are to local citizens.

Before accepting a role as a head of school or its equivalent, the wise leader will review the tenure of the previous heads and seriously consider whether it is prudent to accept a role if the tenures have been short or there has been a very long-serving and much-admired head. Each of these presents different challenges to the new head.

A series of short tenures suggests that relationships between the board members themselves are dysfunctional. The micropolitics between competing groups within a board can change frequently, depending on the issue in hand and the changes to the board membership. Frequent changes of the board chair could be of particular concern for a head, no matter how skilled they are as a leader. The differentials in power will ultimately mean it is unlikely that the head will survive fraught relationships.

If one takes over from a long-serving head who had the respect of the board members, then it becomes difficult to meet the unattainable expectations that established board members may hold, and this will only solidify over time. This situation is prevalent in the small communities that grow around an international school, as parents and staff will use their back channels and influence with board members whenever the new head wishes to make changes in the school.

An international school in Asia had 10 different heads of school in 11 years. It was not the heads who had issues but the board; no matter how skilled the head, they were not going to survive.

CONSTITUTION OF INTERNATIONAL SCHOOL BOARDS

School boards may be made up of parents, professionals, owners or a mixture of different groups with competing agendas. More schools are increasingly being run by a company in the education business and this provides a totally different relationship than that of a school board. All these types of governance provide their own benefits and challenges and the school leader needs to pay specific attention to the relationships between the various factions within the board.

A solely parental board that meets over six times a year should raise immediate red flags. The frequency of meetings would suggest a board that doesn't fully understand its role and perhaps tends to micro-manage the head. Furthermore, if there is no counterweight to the parents' views then the inevitable discussions from playground gossip and WhatsApp conversations will most likely leak into board meetings.

No matter how forcefully parent board members articulate their independence and commitment to the school, they are parents first and friends with parents second. It is better to understand and accept this situation and work with it.

Establish clear guidelines. Don't let a board member's personal anecdote or irritation become the norm in board meeting discussions. Work with the chair to establish guidelines and expectations; create norms of behaviour for board members if needed and make sure that board members sign a conflict-of-interest policy that is regularly reviewed and adhered to.

It is always advantageous to use external support in the form of expert consultants who have worked with many boards when aligning expectations. However, the choice of expert should be delicately agreed with the chair. It is better to propose a few suggested experts to the chair who may not know the educational field. Ensure that your prior relationships with the people you are proposing are transparent; the board is unlikely to accept direction from someone they feel is too closely aligned with the head.

SMALL COMMUNITIES

International school communities are small, intense and fuel gossip and rumour. Accept this as a fact and then manage communications.

The head should actively seek to spot these types of interventions by a board member during board meetings, call them out and seek a private conversation with the relevant board member after the meeting or in the subsequent few days. Informal meetings over a coffee away from the school are a good way to approach sensitive conversations with board members. Of course, this may not be possible. Many board members believe they are high-powered executives and may only be able to spare a short time at their office.

It is not unheard of for a professional conversation between the head and a colleague in school to find its way to a parent. If this parent is friendly with a board member, they might bring this issue up at the next board meeting, thinly veiled as their own agenda. In such instances, asking questions of the board member to ascertain the extent of the issue and the source of the information is a good strategy. One can always agree to meet the board member in the next couple of days to discuss the matter as it is unlikely that the issue will surface again at subsequent meetings.

The minutes of board meetings are crucial for the head as they provide the basis for strategic operations in the school. In many international schools, the board members change frequently and so the head should have a good memory of historical decisions and keep a written note of important decisions that have been agreed at board level, particularly those that have impacted on the school operations.

Bambi Betts from the Principals' Training Center espouses the idea that one should never commit 'assumicide' in any situation. When dealing with boards, it is essential not to jump to conclusions or reveal too much information too quickly. Board members have their own back channels and the astute head will seek to uncover these so that they can articulate their own position during a discussion, in the knowledge that they have the best understanding of the current situation.

BETTER PRACTICES

A good board will support the head, ask relevant and probing questions, understand its responsibilities and duties, while being present in the school community. One of the responsibilities of the board is to set the head's key performance indicators (KPIs). As a minimum, the head should expect to be included in the setting of their own KPIs, through discussion with the appropriate board members, not the whole board. However, both extremes exist from writing one's own KPIs to being provided with them from on high.

The measurement of the head's KPIs is key and this is where the knowing head will reflect carefully on what they agree to before signing the year's goals. Staying away from exam results and student enrolment is preferable but not always possible. Both of these metrics have too many factors outside a head's control; enrolment and results will eventually fall, despite the best efforts of the head and their team.

The better boards meet 3–4 times a year and have 2–4 committees that meet, at most, prior to each board meeting and preferably only if required. The finance committee will usually meet and report back to the main board. The three-way conversation between the finance director/bursar (or equivalent), board treasurer and head is one of the most important triads in the school and one where the head may easily get left behind; a head should insist on being part of those conversations or decisions may inadvertently be made without their consent.

School boards are wonderful entities that can make or break a school and the head. Embrace the challenge and find a trusted confidante to share your frustrations with as there will be many along the journey.

ASIDE

The Principals' Training Center and RSAcademics are two organisations that provide quality board training for international school boards. Here are some questions from the Principals' Training Center[37] that members of your board should be able to answer.

1. What is international school governance actually and what is its purpose?
2. What is, and is not, the work of the board?
3. What are the essential roles, responsibilities and duties of board members?
4. How do you as a board member ensure you are adding value?
5. What are the essential facets of the board—head relationship?
6. What tools does the board have at its disposal to do its work?
7. What are some common pitfalls and biggest surprises you might experience as a new board member?

---

37 The Principals' Training Center. Available at: https://www.theptc.org/

UNITY

Leadership is not just about the actions of one individual; it's about the collective efficacy of the entire school community. When educators believe in their collective ability to positively influence student outcomes, the impact is profound.

John Hattie

The unity of the stakeholders, bringing them together to form a community, is the responsibility of the head. Fostering a sense of belonging to the school provides a rich source of support when times are difficult or when the school needs additional assistance.

One head recalls how they met with over 80 parents in groups of four during the COVID pandemic to listen to their concerns about the school's approach, allay fears, counter gossip and provide reassurance about the upcoming aspects of learning. While the meetings were uncomfortable, the outcomes were significant and the capital gained from the meetings far exceeded everyone's expectations.

Creating inclusive activities and being clear and concise in communication are two essential skills for the international school head. They must be aware of the diverse groups, some of whom may not understand the language of instruction; it is too easy to overlook certain people. A head needs to be intentionally inclusive.

Students in schools with a strong sense of community are more likely to be academically motivated[38] so there is every reason for a head to

---

38 Schaps, E. (2003) 'Creating a school community'. ASCD. Available at: https://www.ascd.org/el/articles/creating-a-school-community

invest their valuable time in this activity. Most parents want to be part of the school community, despite the seemingly endless emails of exaggerated complaints.

Perhaps one of the greatest responsibilities of the head is to focus the community on the future good of the planet. It is through both individual and collective actions that we can realise the future we want, rather than the future we deserve. Education, as always, is the key to success, the key to rectifying the many wrongs of the past.

SHARED RESPONSIBILITY

A head needs to reflect on how to create a shared responsibility between all parties in the school. The challenge for the international head is to cross the cultural and, at times, language barriers that exist within the parent population. The goal is to ensure that every individual member of the community feels a collective responsibility for the school.

Coalescing around a charity event or an inclusive school event is a great way to begin to establish a connectedness. But the event is just the catalyst for enduring involvement of parents in their child's education. Single disconnected activities are like sugar highs, good for the moment but not sustainable for prolonged engagement.

Knowing how to communicate with different cultural groups within the school, and for the class teacher with their students' parents, is a significant factor in fostering the positive relationships that help parents feel valued and, ultimately, connected to the school. The head should liaise with various representative groups within the parent body to ascertain the best ways to reach out to parents. Sometimes the timing of a parent curriculum meeting is a simple starting point that is highly appreciated by working parents.

Similarly with staff, particularly for those new to a school, creating a shared responsibility for success will lead to better outcomes for the students. The inclusive language that is adopted, together with collective responsibility and accountability, establishes the right climate for building a strong community.

The phrase 'building communities' encapsulates the manner in which communities should be perceived. Communities should be built through smaller entities: individual relationships, class gatherings, year group participation, phase-level activities and, finally, school-wide events.

PARTICIPATION

Once a parent, family member or staff member feels connected to the school, then they are far more likely to want to become involved in the school and participate with their heart. This translates not only to participation in events, such as a musical, drama or sporting event, but also with the classroom activities and communication with the teacher about their child's learning.

In most schools, parental involvement tends to diminish as the child enters secondary education. A school must make a conscious decision on how to address this downturn and, indeed, whether it is necessary.

The head needs to participate in as many events as possible, giving credence to the idea that building community is worthy of the head's time.

Creating an ethos during informal and formal interactions at all levels of the family cements the idea of community. Policies could be rewritten to be more family friendly and inclusive. For example, if a student misbehaves to the extent that a parent is asked to attend a meeting, how are these conversations framed? Does the school seek to support and create a tripartite sanction and restorative actions, in which the school, parents and student work together? Or does the school inform parents of the transgression and mete out the punishment?

BUILDING UNITY

There are various well-tested practices that help establish a strong school community. They revolve around communication norms, opportunities to participate meaningfully in the school and a genuine desire for inclusion. A focus on individual partnerships along with school-wide activities will contribute to the glue that binds people in a community.

Respectful relationships

Modelling and insisting on respectful relationships between all members of a school community will establish an open dialogue that one can utilise to make meaningful connections. While there is an inherent hierarchy between students and staff members, and within the organisational structure of the school, this should not impinge on the tone or content of interactions.

Opportunities

One of the big opportunities for an international school is to consciously decide how democratic it wishes to be in its decision-making processes. Different cultures will dictate different approaches. The International Civic and Citizenship Education Study found that Danish students are:[39]

> superior in terms of democratic thinking and citizenship. It also shows that students in Denmark experience an open and anti-authoritarian learning environment where they can comfortably express their opinions.

This comes across strongly in the Danish education system in the way that students are included in the decision-making process and the encouragement that is given to openly question all aspects of student life and have healthy disagreements. Not surprisingly, this democratic process is also manifested in Danish staff employed in international schools and Danish parents who are part of the parent population.

In contrast, some international schools, particularly those with a UK-based curriculum, emphasise 'student voice' as a meaningful way to include students in the decision-making process, but this is rarely embedded into the culture of the school; it is an add-on that could benefit from the Danish approach.

In international studies on happiness, Denmark always appears very high in the rankings. A greater emphasis on democratic collaboration and community decision making in schools may, therefore, be a small step in improving the mental health of the school population.

---

39   International Civic and Citizenship Education Study. Available at: https://iccs.acer.org/

ASIDE

Heads must be vigilant against superficial unity: where appearances are promoted over genuine inclusion, where a lack of cultural sensitivity creates new problems that splinter the community, where the curriculum biases are not addressed, where socioeconomic disparities are not considered in the expectations that schools make of parents' finances. These issues, and the many others that heads are used to managing, lead to a fractured community.

How many schools ask questions of parents in the same vein as the ones below?

1. What is your preferred method of communication?
2. Are there any cultural considerations that you would like to share with us?
3. How can the school best support your family?
4. What level of participation would you like to take within the school community?

VISION

A leader takes people where they want to go. A great leader takes people where they don't necessarily want to go, but ought to be.

Rosalynn Carter

All leaders must be visionary. Without a vision, a leader cannot lead; it is like trying to tack a yacht without a sail – impossible. The vision and values support the school's mission, all of which should be regularly and consistently communicated to all stakeholders.

With quickly changing demographics, an international school leader may have the opportunity to redefine the mission and vision of the school, in conjunction with the board. It is one of the most exciting aspects of leadership: to create an inclusive, shared vision that is noteworthy for the community and has an impact on student learning. Here are some examples of schools' vision and mission statements, taken from schools' websites.

- The UWC movement makes education a force to unite people, nations and cultures for peace and a sustainable future.
- Pioneering education to serve and help shape a better world.
- To challenge and inspire each student to achieve their dreams and to become a passionate learner prepared to adapt and contribute in a rapidly changing world.
- Learning to build community. [We] will develop the potential of each learner by offering educational excellence in a stimulating environment of cultural diversity and mutual respect.
- Education for a Shared Humanity.

They broadly break down into two categories: the descriptive ones that may consist of a couple of sentences to capture the essential elements of the school's intentions and the more succinct types that are easy to remember and contain the nucleus of the school's purpose. The latter kind may be interpreted differently by different members of the community, but this is a strength of the shorter mission statement, as it allows for multiple interpretations within the same theme and it is memorable.

'VISIONING'

Regardless of the mission or vision of the school, the senior leader's job is to bring the vision for the school to life; to be creative and innovative in the approach the school takes to realise the vision and mission agreed in the implicit contract with the community.

Most heads enjoy the creative nature of 'visioning'. The sooner a head understands the freedom they possess to articulate their educational beliefs, the better it is for the school. International school heads should embed their vision in the context of their community that will probably include the culture and traditions of the host country. Not to include this context, particularly with international schools that now have a greater proportion of host-country nationals, will likely cause resentment in the long run.

An inclusive exercise is to involve the entire community in the process of creating the school's intents and strategic priorities. It takes much time to plan and implement, but generates a great deal of positive discussion and all members of the community feel welcomed. It is a great start for a head new to a school, especially if the school has had little change during the recent past.

Along with a vision, the head needs to construct a coherent strategy to deliver the vision. The days of a five-year strategic plan are long gone. Instead schools are adaptive to the volatile, uncertain, complex and ambiguous (VUCA) world in which we live. George proposes a simple mechanism to counter VUCA:[40]

---

40   George, B. (2017) 'VUCA 2.0: A strategy for steady leadership in an unsteady world'. Available at: https://www.forbes.com/sites/hbsworkingknowledge/2017/02/17/vuca-2-0-a-strategy-for-steady-leadership-in-an-unsteady-world/#1a6e660a13d8

- volatility with vision
- uncertainty with understanding
- complexity with courage
- ambiguity with adaptability.

STRATEGIC INTENTS AND PRIORITIES

One such way to develop the school's strategic direction is to agree to some high-level strategic intents that capture the essence of the school's purpose. It is likely that between five and ten are required to cover all aspects of the school. From these intents, annual, whole-school strategic priorities may be developed; perhaps between three and five are manageable, although there are always exceptions. Fewer than three could indicate either a lack of ambition or that the strategic priorities are too condensed. More than five become unmanageable.

For each strategic priority, a whole-school action plan is developed that provides details of targets, timelines, resources, success criteria and, importantly, who is to lead on each target and who is to monitor each target.

These whole-school action plans then cascade down to phase-level action plans and year-level or department-level action plans.

EXAMPLES OF STRATEGIC INTENTS

Intent 1

We will develop and implement an inspirational Future Ready Curriculum that provides an exceptional education, preparing students to be role models for the world.

Intent 2

We will be a world leader in understanding and applying the evolving body of evidence about effective learning and teaching.

Intent 3

We will foster the talents and aspirations of students in the arts and sport, enabling students to reach their potential, with some able to participate at the elite or professional level in their chosen area of expertise.

Examples of Strategic Priorities are found in Section Two.

Each of the strategic priorities will have its own action plan, the key elements of which are best captured in a table.

Knowing *how* the senior team will go about making the changes is as important as the changes they will make. Again, so much is written about change management, but in the international context, it is imperative that senior leaders take into account the frequency of staff turnover when devising and implementing change.

DECLUTTERING

How many schools review their processes and procedures and actively decide to stop doing something, rather than letting it fade away? Decluttering school operations is as important as adding new initiatives. There is a finite amount of time available and schools are masters of accumulated processes. The excellent book by Hamilton, Hattie and

Wiliam[41] puts forward strategies for school leaders to pursue strategic de-implementation. According to Hamilton *et al.*, three key reasons to de-implement are:

- to save time, reduce teacher workload and stress, improve teacher wellbeing
- to save financial resources
- to reinvest time and resources into high-impact activities.

As leaders review strategic priorities, they must also take time to declutter the school of activities, processes and policies that have no positive impact on student learning; to remove the fragments of forgotten or disregarded ideas that still exist within the school's ecosystem. This is, of course, a major exercise as the school would need to measure the impact of all its operations.

VUCA

Volatile, uncertain, complex and ambiguous (VUCA) times will require confident leadership that is flexible and solution-focused. It is neither possible nor desirable to plan for all eventualities and when the terrain changes quickly, a leader must first recognise the change and then respond accordingly.

The growing business of international schools has transformed the educational offering in numerous countries across the world. Established international schools face stronger competition. School groups target opportunities and can set up schools in a new country almost overnight; their well-practised and well-financed marketing machines swing into operation and transform the once-cosy educational offerings. Competing in these circumstances cannot rely on past performance.

---

41 Hamilton, A., Hattie, J. and Wiliam, D. (2023) *Making Room for Impact: A De-implementation Guide for Educators.* Corwin: California, USA.

ASIDE

As we evolve and exploit the world, we will need to empower students with *agency*: the ability to understand the world, have a shared sense of responsibility to engage with the world, and lead others to create a better world. International schools with their diverse populations, involved parents and geographical locations are ideally placed to challenge students, parents and teachers so that students leave with agency.

What changes would a school leader have to make so that students:

- had a comprehensive understanding of the world – the interconnectedness of its peoples and resources
- felt a genuine responsibility for self and others
- had the knowledge, skills and personal characteristics, so that they could lead others to create an infinitesimally better world?

WELLBEING

States Parties recognize the right of the child to the enjoyment of the highest attainable standard of health and to facilities for the treatment of illness and rehabilitation of health ...'

The UN Convention on the Rights of the Child, Article 24

Which school would not agree to the UN Convention on the Rights of the Child, even if the country in which the school is based does not agree to all or some of the UN articles? How many schools actively promote the UN rights of the child in their educational offering, in the way in which their policies and procedures are articulated and actioned? If all schools committed and acted on their commitment to the UN Convention on the Rights of the Child then children's wellbeing would be immeasurably enhanced.

Wellbeing is a contemporary form of care, which essentially supersedes pastoral care that is founded in the spiritual care of organised religion. In schools, wellbeing encompasses the support that is provided to staff, but more importantly to students. A greater emphasis and focus on wellbeing has occurred over the past few decades in national and international schools, resulting in much research and guidance about how schools can enhance their wellbeing provision.

Since the usual pattern for attendance at school is at least five hours or more a day, five days a week, it feels right that this heavy responsibility of student wellbeing is shared between parents and schools, particularly since schools are the causes of some of the traumas that students experience. Of course, there are variations of the school day with some students by necessity spending less time at school and others, such as boarding students, spending significantly more time at school.

The international school leader should make it clear that wellbeing is a shared responsibility, with parents taking the main responsibility, even if the parents are not as focused or as active as the school. Article 18 of the UN Convention on the Rights of the Child states:

> Parents or, as the case may be, legal guardians, have the primary responsibility for the upbringing and development of the child. The best interests of the child will be their basic concern.

Cultural sensitivities dictate a nuanced approach when discussing wellbeing with parents. However, child protection issues must always be addressed.

Mental health is one aspect of wellbeing that receives greater attention for obvious reasons. The pressures that students now face seem appreciably greater than the pressures faced by students a generation ago.

The interconnectedness of the world and easier access to higher education and careers across different countries mean students are competing on a global scale rather than just nationally. International schools, originated to support these mobile families, are now educating more local families and are, consequently, a contributor to the idea that students can attend any university, anywhere in the world. Students at international schools (and their parents) expect to compete on a global scale. This places an emphasis on increased academic competition, exacerbated by social media.

The very fact that there is a greater awareness and emphasis on wellbeing and mental health mitigates some of these issues but levels of engagement will vary dramatically from school to school, country to country. School counsellors play an important role in preventing, supporting and destigmatising mental health issues. Increased acceptance of the diversity, equity and inclusion discourse also helps alleviate some wellbeing issues.

DEFINITIONS

As the literature around wellbeing has exploded, it is necessary for schools to develop their own working definition of wellbeing. Here is one such definition based on Seligman's PERMA model[42].

> Wellbeing is our overall sense of health, happiness and life satisfaction. It is not a permanent state of happiness, but rather a state in which we can cope with the stresses and difficulties of daily life. The pursuit of positive wellbeing enables us to flourish.

It is important to note that it is an individual's responsibility to promote their own health and recognise how the following aspects of health affect our overall wellbeing.

Mental health. This refers to a sense of fulfilment and the ability to manage daily stresses in order to perform key functions. This includes:

- having the capacity to learn and grow; keeping problems in perspective and being able to recover from setbacks; adapting to change and coping with uncertainty; managing stressful situations and personal anxieties. This also improves self-motivation and perseverance, both of which are necessary for success.

Emotional health. This refers to our ability to control our thoughts, feelings and behaviours. This includes:

- feeling good about ourselves and having an optimistic/realistic outlook; having good self-awareness and regulating positive and negative emotions. This also increases our capacity for self-reflection and resilience as a learner.

Social health. This refers to our ability to communicate with others and form positive interpersonal relationships. This includes:

- developing friendships; relating to and communicating with others; having a sense of belonging and connectedness; feeling secure in your own company; and being able to adapt to new social situations. This also improves our emotional intelligence and cultivates empathy for others.

---

42   Madeson, M. (2017) 'Seligman's PERMA+ model explained: A theory of wellbeing'. PositivePsychology.com. Available at: https://positivepsychology.com/perma-model/

Physical health. This refers to the extent that we feel physically safe and healthy. This includes:

- eating a balanced diet, exercising on a regular basis, engaging in preventative health care, getting adequate sleep, avoiding harmful substances and feeling secure. This also increases our energy and alertness.

WELLBEING MODELS

Some simple steps that schools could adopt to enhance wellbeing.

1. Create or adapt a wellbeing model that works in your context. This is especially true for international school leaders.

2. Ensure staff are trained in how best to support their students. Most of the time this is taken for granted, and not perceived as an integral part of a teacher's responsibility. In international schools, staff are more likely to have diverse experiences which can bring both positive and negative elements to a school.

3. Create a culture where diversity is celebrated and inclusion is normalised. Challenge the negative stereotypes.

4. Educate the entire community about positive health and how this can be achieved; do not take simple things for granted, such as that people know what a good diet looks like or how much sleep is sufficient.

5. Ensure that counsellors are visible and part of the day-to-day operations of the school.

There are various models and approaches to wellbeing from which international schools may choose. Four such models are very briefly outlined below.

Positive Education Model[43]

This model is based on positive psychology and related fields, looking at building character strengths and a sense of purpose. Geelong Grammar School in Australia is known for its wellbeing programme based on positive psychology.

---

43 Positive Education. Available at: https://www.ipen-network.com/about-us

Social and emotional learning[44]

Social and emotional learning is concerned with specific interventions that focus on improving social interactions as well as managing emotional responses.

The PERMA Model

This was developed by Seligman and can be briefly summarised as follows: increasing positive emotions, engaging with an activity in the moment, being involved in relationships where one feels supported, loved and valued by others, finding meaning or purpose in life, and feeling one has accomplished something through perseverance and challenge.

The Flourish Model[45]

The Flourish Model is a way to understand the physical, emotional, mental and spiritual aspects of what it is to be human. There is an emphasis on community involvement and creating a more sustainable world.

---

44 Collaborative for Academic, Social, and Emotional Learning. Available at: https://casel.org/about-us/
45 The Flourish Model. Available at: https://www.flourishproject.net/

ASIDE

Senior leaders need to practise what they preach, and look after their own wellbeing.

1. What is the right work–life balance for you? Bear in mind that there are numerous studies about the inefficiencies of spending too much time working, and that you would probably spend at least half of your working life in a senior leadership role.

2. What do you do to disconnect from work? Is this a creative, physical, intellectual or social pursuit, or perhaps a combination of these?

3. Do you build thinking time into your day?

4. How do you promote the wellbeing of those that you lead?

5. Who is your confidante?

XENAGOGUE

Leaders have to provide direction, create the conditions for effective peer interaction, and intervene along the way when things are not working as well as they could.

Michael Fullan

The international leader is a xenagogue for the community. They guide policy, set the tone in communication, provide a long-term, global perspective as the school explores the educational landscape, and they dispense intellectual and emotional sustenance for the school.

The head leads the school on a journey of growth and improvement, often over an extended period of time. They navigate obstacles and choose their travelling companions in the form of partnerships with local companies, global charities and NGOs.

The initial year for a head will be one of clarity, when a new head can see the issues and celebrate the exceptional. This is a time for honest reflection and setting the agenda for the next few years. The moments of clarity will diminish as the landscape becomes familiar and loses its immediacy. The head is soon institutionalised and has to take greater and greater responsibility for the school, so that the problems that existed when the head arrived cease to be the previous head's issues, but firmly become the new head's problems and responsibility.

A senior leader must be clear about their own values; these will guide and, at times, restrict decisions that are made. The most intractable problems will often require the head to make a judgement call, which can only be based on their own values and principles.

CULTURAL JOURNEY

For many heads who move to a new country, navigating the new cultural landscape is enlightening and fulfilling, on both a personal level and a professional level. It will provide a rich source of opportunities to review the curriculum.

However, there will be challenges. For example, if the school is located in a country where alcohol is prohibited, how does one prepare older students for life after school at a university in a country where alcohol is prevalent? A head who worked in the Middle East sensitively asked parents of sixth form students to opt into a series of talks about such culturally inflammatory issues as consent and sensible alcohol consumption. Only around 50% opted into the talks.

The OECD included interculturalism in their PISA (Programme for International Student Assessment) 2018 Global Competence assessment.[46]

> The PISA 2018 Global Competence assessment measures students' capacity to examine local, global and intercultural issues, to engage in open, appropriate and effective interactions with people from different cultures, and to act for collective well-being and sustainable development.

Global competence can help young people:

- develop cultural awareness and respectful interactions in increasingly diverse societies;
- recognise and challenge cultural biases and stereotypes, and facilitate harmonious living in multicultural communities;
- prepare for the world of work, which increasingly demands individuals who are effective communicators, are open to people from different cultural backgrounds, can build trust in diverse teams and can demonstrate respect for others, especially as technology continues to make it easier to connect on a global scale;

---

46 OECD PISA 2018 Global Competence. Available at: https://www.oecd.org/pisa/innovation/global-competence/

- capitalise on inherently interconnected digital spaces, question biased media representations, and express their voice responsibly online;
- care about global issues and engage in tackling social, political, economic and environmental challenges.

International schools with an engaged head who believes in the worth of global competencies have a great advantage over schools with monocultures. The richness of cultures and ethnicities that can be investigated is immense, and provides learning opportunities that cannot be bought online.

PROFESSIONAL JOURNEY

Travelling with fellow professionals, and choosing who these may be, is more important than travelling alone. No head knows everything, despite what they may tell you or have you believe. Of course, heads need to be well versed in pedagogy, operations, HR practices, etc. but much is learned on a need-to-use basis. If a new sports hall is to be built, then pull together a team of consultants and ask pertinent questions. About to employ a graphic designer into the marketing team, then review their work and ask them to provide three designs for an upcoming school show.

As an international leader moves to a new country, they will discover new landscapes. Their ability to quickly grasp the intricacies of a new labour law, for example, is an aspect that requires almost immediate attention, since the issues the head deals with invariably come around to continued employment of a staff member, and the sooner a head knows the parameters in which they are operating, the easier it is for them to plan accordingly.

PERSONAL JOURNEY

Adapting and re-adapting to an ever-changing environment is one of the most rewarding parts of international school leadership. Most heads will be on their own personal journey that is private. This should always include developing their professional expertise, but will also involve managing the personal side of their lives while running the school. Their personal life may be about learning a new skill or supporting their family. Some heads share elements of their personal life with a few confidantes, others keep it private. No matter what the head's personal journey entails, it is still expected that they will keep the personal separate from the professional.

But is this right? Will there be a time when we accept or even expect leaders to share pertinent details of their private life? If their child was gravely ill in hospital, surely this would contextualise their working life? And if this type of occurrence is shared, what about other details? Where is the line drawn and is the boundary shifting?

Whatever the approach a head takes, most understand that the journey is long and their personal wellbeing is their own responsibility. It is very unlikely that a board member will look out for their mental health, unless the head is managing a significant crisis. Exercise or music, friends or family, each head must find their own release from the job. It is too much to ask of a head to make quality decisions and consistently produce high-quality work if they are constantly tired and drained.

TRAGIC JOURNEY

Navigating new cultures and experiences is challenging, especially if this involves dealing with the death of a student; even more so if this is suicide. Anecdotal conversations would suggest that this sorrowful event occurs far too often.

One head recalls how they were informed of a student suicide one evening. The head was over 5000 km away from the school at an educational conference. They could not meaningfully engage with the immediate incident and support the student's family and affected colleagues, nor easily turn to their own family for comfort. Another head was informed about a student suicide in the middle of a meeting. While another recalls the two years of legal wranglings that they had to deal with when a student at their school committed suicide on the school premises. The latter, involving lawyers over a protracted period of time, was particularly demanding on the head and their family.

No one wants to have to deal with these situations, but it is a matter of probability that at some point during a long career a head will face such a situation. One of the heads recalls that while attending the funeral of their ex-student, the family extended their gratitude to the school, and personally to the head, by allowing the head to view the uncovered body. An instant decision was made by the head who knew that, out of respect, they had to view the body of the deceased student.

After liaising with the family, if they permit such communication, the next step would be to inform, in confidence, those staff members and students who may be significantly traumatised by the event. Agreeing a communication plan with the family is difficult but important. Some families may ask for the school to delay any announcement of their child's death until the family has contacted their own relatives. The school may want to agree at this stage that if the news is leaked onto social media, which is highly likely, then the school would have to make an announcement, so preparing communication to the staff, students and parents is critical.

Once the tragic news has been released, continued communication with the family and affected people, use of school counsellors, perhaps the secondment of counsellors from neighbouring schools, planning for a memorial and attending the funeral are all events that should be considered. But it will not be until the head has to deal with such a terrible incident that they will know the right course of action; these events cannot be planned in detail in advance because they do not follow a predetermined path.

ASIDE

What personal characteristics are a must and what are nice to have for a leader? Are certain characteristics more or less important for international school leaders? Is it possible to rank order or at least create 3–5 groups of the most important attributes required for a leader from the list below?

courage   resilience   flexibility

integrity   transparent communication

empathy   confidence   passion

influence   compassion   a sense of social justice

self-awareness   loyalty   optimism

strategic thinking   analytical thinking

caring   decisive decision-maker   responsible

vision   humility   respect

drive   active listener   motivator

delegator   innovator   cultural sensitivity

emotional intelligence   creative   honesty

YOKED

Leaders create leaders by passing on responsibility, creating ownership, accountability and trust. The challenge is to always improve, to always get better, even when you are the best.

James Kerr

The term yoked conjures up images of oxen in a field, pulling on a heavy plough as they strain to turn the earth, preparing the ground in another annual cycle. However, if we allow a little creative licence and imagine horses or even huskies harnessed, the metaphor becomes more agile, faster paced, determined and focused.

Of all teams in a school, the senior leaders should be the most tightly yoked, moving in unison with energy and purpose.

The head's role is to manage and lead this group of individuals who are often creative, intelligent, articulate and, in equal measure, frustrating, annoying and stubborn.

Most medium to large schools will have someone with overall responsibility for the school. Schools with co-heads are, at present, very much in the minority. The title for the person in charge varies between different cultures but includes: principal, head of school, head, superintendent, president and director, to name a few.

THE SENIOR TEAM STRUCTURE

Reporting to the head will be the next senior educational administrators who will likely be responsible for phases of the school, grouped by student age range. Then there will probably be a few others who are part of the senior team that may cover the roles of finance, operations, marketing, development, IT, plus a few others depending on the needs of the school.

Having established who the head wants to be part of the senior team, making executive decisions, the next decision for the head is how to manage the team.

Some heads prefer to have large meetings with the whole of the top team so that all aspects of the school are covered in decision making. Others prefer to break the team into smaller constituents. The key point here is to recognise that there is a choice for the head to make, to decide how they would like to operate. It is perfectly possible to start with one structure and then move to another. And this depends on what they wish to achieve. Simon Sinek[47] comments that you always start with the 'why'. So the head needs to know their own 'why'. Why are they pursuing a particular strategy? Why do they want to change the structure of the school day? Why does the head want a particular senior leadership team structure; what will the changes achieve and how will it achieve its goals?

The head will need to decide how to structure meetings with the executive team. To carry on with the same routines as the previous head is to implicitly say that you have the same 'why' questions, which is highly unlikely.

A head should also decide how much operational 'stuff' to manage in a meeting; how much time and effort should be spent on strategy? Inevitably, there will be crises that arise from time to time. Setting goals and keeping the team yoked, ensuring alignment across phases where necessary but allowing difference and individuality when appropriate, are all valuable actions for the head to pursue. Section Two contains a helpful diagnostic tool that allows the head to analyse a team's effectiveness.

Managing the agenda for the executive team sets the tone for the school. Meaningful agendas take time and careful planning. It is worth the head giving reflective time to the weekly agendas.

---

47   Sinek, S. (2009) *Start With Why: How Great Leaders Inspire Everyone to Take Action.* New York: Penguin Group (USA) Inc.

MICROMANAGEMENT

No senior leader wants to be micromanaged. But there is a difference between intervening when something is wrong and micromanaging a person. Getting this right is crucial to the success of the relationship, and the outcomes for the school.

Communication, collaboration and courage

Most leaders will have examples where miscommunication has led to further calamities. International school leaders need to avoid cultural assumptions around communication, which are far too easy to make. For example, in some cultures it is considered polite to infer or ask questions rather than be direct and blunt, but unless the person receiving the message understands the delicate nuances of a particular culture, it will be lost and chaos will ensue.

Most senior leaders acknowledge the need to collaborate, whether to reach the best decision or produce the highest-quality documents. There is so much to do that it cannot be done by one person or a small team, therefore collaboration is imperative. It is best to be deliberate about this collaboration and empower the right people.

Disagreement is guaranteed in leadership, otherwise poor outcomes are assured. It may take courage from a head to make an unpopular decision, to advocate for a student who has almost reached the end of the road, to support a staff member whom one of the senior leaders wishes to be fired.

SINGLE MINDEDNESS

Single mindedness in senior leaders is a trait that can be harnessed for positive outcomes but, if left unchecked, it can result in divergence of purpose, lack of respect between colleagues and, inevitably, poor communication.

Some senior leaders in charge of a school age phase may perceive the head to be interfering in something they know little about. There may be tensions between other age phase leaders, they might be totally focused on their next career move, they may subtly follow their own agenda rather than an agreed, shared direction. Worse still, there may be a narcissist, an aggressive control freak, among the senior leaders.

No matter who the phase leaders and other senior leaders are they will need to be managed, and kept moving in the same direction. If the head gets the right culture within the senior team and manages to sustain this culture, not as easy as it sounds, then the rest of the work will flow relatively smoothly, even when tackling the thorniest of challenges.

The appraisal process, or equivalent, is a key driver for success at the senior level and, in order to keep a tightly yoked team, it is something to which the head should dedicate time and energy. Regularly reviewing the KPIs or goals that have been mutually agreed at the beginning of the year refreshes everyone's memories and brings a focus back to the team. This mechanism allows the head to adjust attitudes and approaches, not just review tasks that a senior leader may be developing, contrary to the head's wishes.

ACKNOWLEDGE GREATNESS

It is unlikely that the head will be the most knowledgeable in the senior team about all things educational. Recognising the strengths and expertise of others in the team is a key leadership attribute. It comes naturally to some, but is a concept that escapes others. In general, heads do not require external recognition for their work in order to thrive; it is unlikely they would have become a head if this was a requirement. Consequently, some heads refrain from providing direct or indirect praise as a motivating factor for others, since it was not a key element in their own progression. Where are you as a senior leader on the continuum of praise-giving?

Writing for the *Harvard Business Review*[48], Robbins comments on both recognition and appreciation for employees, making a distinction between the two, with recognition being performance based while appreciation is about the inherent worth of an individual.

> In simple terms, recognition is about what people do; appreciation is about who they are.

48 Robbins, M. (2019) 'Why employees need both recognition and appreciation'. *Harvard Business Review*. Available at: https://hbr.org/2019/11/why-employees-need-both-recognition-and-appreciation

Each head should know their own strengths and weaknesses and how the team can complement each other. Delegation of challenging responsibilities or areas that might be deemed the head's realm is a great way to reward others, acknowledge expertise and create a stronger connection with a senior leader. It also relieves some of the work pressures of the head.

ANALYTICAL AND SYSTEMS THINKING

The issues that a senior school leader has to solve are complex and require careful and sustained thinking. Both systems and analytical thinking together give the senior leader a powerful approach to understand the challenges they face. Note it is often better to view the situation as a challenge to overcome rather than a problem to solve, as rarely does a leader find *the* solution. There are often many possible futures that exist, and the one that ultimately emerges will generally require flexibility from all parties coupled with close monitoring of progress and support from the head.

Reference to the shared moral purpose, either explicitly or implicitly, is helpful in difficult situations but not always sufficient to find an agreed direction. On many occasions, the moral purpose needs to be stripped back to the very core aspiration and the head is often required to make a definitive decision. But a decision after a discussion around moral purpose is far better than a decision in the cold without context or rationale. Fullan[49] writes:

> Moral purpose is the link between system thinking and sustainability ... meeting the goals of moral purpose produces commitment throughout the system.

Heads who understand Fullan's observation will be able to keep a tightly yoked team of senior leaders moving forwards in a cohesive manner, almost in unison.

A system is where the constituent parts are intimately connected. Change one part of the system and the others change too; causality is

---

49 Fullan, M. (2004) *Leadership & Sustainability: System Thinkers in Action*. Corwin Press and Ontario Principals' Council.

an important feature of systems. By combining systems thinking for the whole with an analytical approach to the individual parts, it is possible to better understand the challenge.

Consider an errant senior leader who is part of the executive team, but disregards agreements that have been reached with the team. It is impossible to disentangle the senior leader's actions from the context of the team dynamics and the interpersonal relationships, as well as the singular goals of the errant leader within their own professional context. By looking at the system as a whole, and analysing the parts and their connectedness, the head can begin to understand better how to realign the team, not just the errant leader. Perhaps the personal relationship between the errant leader and another team member is fraught, or the errant leader has pressures from the staff whom they lead, or they have a long history of getting their own way, or ... .

It is impossible to simply focus on the errant senior leader as a means to overcome the challenge.

ASIDE

Is there a happy medium when it comes to praising someone? What effect does criticism have on employees' performance? Stocker et al.[50] talk about appreciative behaviours and describe six categories: praise and gratitude; trust and responsibility; support and respect; motivated cooperation; tangible reward and promotion; no behaviour specified.

On average they found that employees received approximately one appreciative behaviour a day, with the category praise and gratitude being the most frequently used. However, while appreciation by leaders is important, the sense of wellbeing in employees was raised just as much when praised by co-workers.

So, school leaders should ensure they create a culture of appreciation among all employees and use the full range of appreciative behaviours.

To what extent do you agree with the following statements?

1. Staff are paid for the work they do; they need to get on with it without all the external acknowledgements that some seem to need.

2. It is damaging to overpraise an individual as the sentiment loses value. In the same vein, if one individual is frequently praising many employees, then the praise from that individual loses value and meaning, because that is what they become known for – praising others.

3. Praise can lead to an inflated sense of self, thus having a negative impact on the rest of the team.

4. Praise is the key method to demonstrate that you care for other employees.

5. Giving praise is a key motivator for employees and should be planned and mapped by leaders.

---

50 Stocker, D. et al. (2014) 'Appreciative leadership and employee well-being in everyday working life'. Zeitschrift für Personalforschung/German Journal of Research in Human Resource Management. 28(1/2): pp. 73–95. Available at: http://www.jstor.org/stable/24332803

ZEITGEIST

As-salaam Alaikum

Jacinda Ardern

A few days after the two mosque attacks in Christchurch on 15 March 2019, where 51 people were killed, Jacinda Ardern addressed the New Zealand people at a memorial service with the Islamic greeting 'As-salaam Alaikum', meaning 'peace be upon you'.

With this phrase and her immediate, genuine outpouring of love for the families who had lost relatives in the horrific attacks, she was able to connect instantly both with these traumatised people and with millions of others around the world who craved a different type of leadership.

Ardern led New Zealand's response to the massacre, having genuinely felt moved by the horrific events, and she allowed this to be part of her public response. Her empathy allowed her compassion to shine strong. Not only was she authentic in her response but her authenticity was exactly what the world needed at the time and still needs. It is no use being your authentic self if your authenticity is out of kilter with most of those you are leading.

CONTEXTUAL AUTHENTICITY

Zeitgeist leadership is about having the right personal qualities to lead during the events and spirit of the time. Did Ardern emerge as a great leader because her personal qualities matched the moment in history? Or did she shape the public discourse of leadership through her intellect and personal qualities? Perhaps she seized the moment because she recognised the zeitgeist. Undoubtedly, the interconnectedness and intersection of multiple factors will have played a role.

Mayo and Nohria, in the *Harvard Business Review*,[51] discuss the merits of Welch as the, then new, CEO of General Electric. He understood the zeitgeist and was able to turn around the fortunes of the company.

In our current climate, authentic leadership is part of zeitgeist leadership, but being authentic is not enough. Our world is being torn apart with the rise of nationalism and ideologies that fracture societies. As I write, wars are raging in Europe, the Middle East, Africa and Asia. An alternative world view is required by all sane leaders. Inclusive, empathetic, compassionate leadership, complemented by a fierce intelligence and a deep understanding of our times, all combine to provide hope; hope for humanity in these darkening days.

Zeitgeist leadership is about leading for the context of the times, being able to connect to the spirit and foresee the new trends. Schools are responding more quickly than ever to societal changes and technological innovation. It is expected that schools utilise the latest educational research in their restless pursuit of excellence.

Leadership today is about contextual authenticity – feeling and believing in the zeitgeist, tempered by a strong sense of moral justice.

CHARACTERISTICS OF ZEITGEIST LEADERSHIP

Being able to look to the future is possible when the present is taken care of, so empowerment of teams and appropriate delegation are key characteristics of a zeitgeist leader. This will create time for reflection and allow the international school leader to synthesise the current, swirling milieu of ideas and understand the vibe of the community and country.

In the current climate, coaching and mentoring are key elements of the zeitgeist leader. Delegation of decision making, rather than completion of tasks, will engage employers with the heart and foster personal growth. Of course, delegation is not a free-for-all activity; it requires the head

---

51   Mayo, A.J. and Nohria, N. (2005) 'Zeitgeist leadership'. *Harvard Business Review*. Available at: https://hbr.org/2005/10/zeitgeist-leadership

to know their staff, to know the envelope of their capabilities and allow them to develop, explore and fail safely.

Many of the school leaders who led through the COVID pandemic would require a different set of attributes: decisive decisions, agile responses and creative approaches to overcome some of the many obstacles they faced. But the most important detail for most leaders at that time was to understand how their community was coping with the times; to feel the loss, the anguish, the desperate hope for the pandemic to end. Thus, empathy is the most important attribute for a zeitgeist leader.

HIRING THE NEXT GENERATION

The zeitgeist leader enjoys the process of selecting and hiring staff. They will fully understand the needs of people, will already have instigated improvements in their current school and will always have exciting plans for the next few academic years. A head's enthusiasm and descriptions of the possible futures for prospective candidates will enthral them and raise their professional expectations.

An open discussion about the merits of a particular learning strategy or leadership approach will enable the head to discern the degree of engagement with, and understanding of, educational concepts that the candidates possess.

Appreciating the differences and similarities[52] in expectations between different generations, while a generalisation, will aid the head in the hiring process. Is the head looking for independent workers or collaborative colleagues, digital natives or digital explorers, role-focused or job-focused candidates, career-minded people or those wanting a healthy work–life balance? These are generalised assumptions between millennials and generation Zers, but provide a loose focus for the hiring head who might be looking to establish a new culture or fill a gap in their staffing profile.

---

52 'Millennials and Gen Z in the workplace: similarities and differences'. Available at: https://eures.europa.eu/millennials-and-gen-z-workplace-similarities-and-differences-2023-03-02_en

EDUCATIONAL TRENDS

Some recent societal changes have been mirrored in schools. For example, a school's focus on diversity, equity and inclusion follows the movements taking place across Western workplaces, and the polarised public and political discourse. The tightening of how schools manage data more effectively has been driven by the change in laws in Europe and other countries. The explosion of artificial intelligence is already part of the mainstream discussions in schools.

But what is coming next?

No doubt climate changes will increase at a faster and faster pace until we are unable to avoid taking drastic action. The current public debate on climate change has normalised the extreme weather conditions and numbed our senses; we are 'comfortably numb'. This is exacerbated by irresponsible politicians who trade dangerous rhetoric for votes.

In a move to counter terrorism, the UK government introduced statutory guidance for schools in their 'prevent' strategy. Recent updates came into force in December 2023. While countering terrorism is one thing, further legislation on social issues could easily be introduced into national UK schools. This would quickly find its way into international schools, through educational standards and UK staff being hired for international schools, particularly since British education is the most prolific of all international curricula. As we consider future government interventions it is worth bearing in mind that section 28 (a law that banned schools and local authorities from 'promoting homosexuality') was introduced into UK schools in 1988, then repealed in 2003. Where will new legislation go as nationalism rises and social acceptance of difference becomes even more divergent?

Schools are not the best users of data. As institutions they generate so much data, the security of which still needs to improve, but learning could be significantly enhanced if schools were able to manage and analyse much larger datasets. In the same way that educational research is part of mainstream education, the use of large datasets will become ubiquitous.

Individualised learning pathways should become more prominent. The current model of education lacks imagination in its offerings. Blended learning may return where schools partner with other schools in different geographical locations. The use of technology to access opportunities across the globe and create bespoke curricula is very exciting, and international schools are ideally placed to lead this transformation. And, of course, the explosion of AI will revolutionise education, both in pedagogy and assessment.

While schools endeavour to remain apolitical, the increasing polarisation and political extremes that we are now witnessing through the mainstream media, driven by the intrusion of social media into our lives, could eventually force schools to be more explicit in their political alignment. Heads may need to be clear about their own political views, as they are the figurehead of the school. Or maybe schools will move to more co-leadership positions where differing political views are held by multiple heads and shared with the community in a bid to present a balanced perspective. For international schools, a move in this direction would be almost impossible to manage with their very diverse communities and local laws, so perhaps international schools would remain apolitical.

Whatever the future holds, it is incumbent on international school leaders to provide an education that looks beyond the immediate, takes a historical perspective to frame the present, and provides contextual leadership for a truly shared humanity.

ASIDE

How much do you agree with the statements below about the future of education?

1. Students will create their own educational pathways.
2. Innovation and creativity, entrepreneurship and collaboration will be central elements of the curriculum.
3. Older students will work from home for a portion of each week, utilising technology in their learning.
4. Students will be able to select their teachers, mentors or coaches.
5. Artificial intelligence, augmented reality and gamification of learning will form the basis for all future learning strategies.

SECTION TWO

SECTION
TWO

STRATEGIC INTENTS

Annual strategic priorities will be developed to reach these long term strategic intents. These intents provide direction and encourage empathy as we continually strive for excellence.

INTENT 1
We will confirm, make explicit and strengthen the **one-school culture** in which a seamless education is offered from Nursery to the Sixth Form

INTENT 2
We will build a **technology-rich environment** for students, staff and parents as one enabler of learning

INTENT 3
We will develop and implement an **Inspirational Future Ready Curriculum** that provides an exceptional education, preparing students to be role models for the world

INTENT 4
We will be a world leader in understanding and **applying the evolving body of evidence** about effective learning and teaching

INTENT 5
We will be a learning organisation in which everybody is **passionate about learning** with an abundance of supporting evidence found in our school and community

INTENT 6
We will put in place the buildings, infrastructure and other resources for St Christopher's to be a **world-class school**

INTENT 7
We will have **clear internal and external communications** between all **stakeholders** and dialogue and feedback will enlighten and inform school development

INTENT 8
We will **establish caring relationships** between all members of the St Christopher's community where all are expected to meet the highest expectations and be held individually accountable for his or her contributions

INTENT 9
We will **foster the talents and aspirations of students** in the Arts and Sport, enabling them to participate at the elite or professional level in their chosen area of expertise

INTENT 10
We will create the culture and practices that support the **successful implementation of these strategic intents, our mission, vision, values and the curriculum** in its widest context

Education for a Shared Humanity

@stchrisbahrain

181

STRATEGIC PRIORITIES

STRATEGIC PRIORITIES 2023/24

FUTURE READY CURRICULUM
The School will continue to develop and embed the Future Ready Curriculum into the ethos of St Christopher's.

PROFESSIONAL LEARNING
The School will use Professional Development Portfolios and its Professional Learning Programme to engage, inspire and equip staff to develop successfully as outstanding practitioners.

TEACHING, LEARNING & ASSESSMENT
The School will continue to identify and embed effective pedagogical practice from the Pedagogical Rubric and related research, as well as emerging practice from the Future Ready Curriculum competencies and Hybrid teaching.

CULTURE AND CLIMATE
The School will aspire to create a climate and culture in which all members of St Christopher's community flourish.

Education for a Shared Humanity

 @stchrisbahrain

PEDAGOGICAL RUBRIC

It is expected that not all elements from the pedagogical rubric (based on Rosenshine's principles) are met within a single lesson visit. However, over a period of time, it is expected that all elements are met. There are four possible categories for the individual descriptors within the pedagogical rubric:

- Instructor – the teacher has mastered this element of the rubric and is able to conduct CPD in this area and support colleagues.
- Confident – the teacher is confident in their own practice of this element but further consolidation is required before they conduct CPD and support colleagues.
- Not observed – this element has not yet been observed or demonstrated by the teacher.
- Not yet met – the teacher has tried to demonstrate this element but has not yet met the confident descriptor.

REVIEWING MATERIAL	
Confident	**Instructor**
The teacher begins most lessons with a short review of previous learning (including homework where appropriate). Clear links are made between new and previous learning. Students are given opportunities to overlearn new skills, knowledge and concepts.	The teacher is especially adept at identifying the skills, knowledge and concepts and instilling the attitude that students will need to master. Careful planning of the consolidation of new skills and concepts is evident in all lessons.

Within and across units, the teacher provides frequent opportunities through formal and informal assessments for students to review previous learning.	The teacher has established a structured system of review in which students regularly consolidate previous learning and apply it in new and unfamiliar contexts.
QUESTIONING AND CONSOLIDATING/CHECKING FOR UNDERSTANDING	
Confident	**Instructor**
The teacher asks a variety of open and closed questions which are differentiated in most cases. Students are expected to explain, clarify or justify their responses with appropriate levels of sophistication.	The teacher's questioning strategies are very well developed, both in terms of the range of techniques used and their impact on the students' learning.
The teacher regularly checks the students' understanding of instructions and concepts, and students' responses often inform the pace and course of a lesson.	The teacher involves all students when clarifying or extending their understanding, and students' responses consistently inform the pace and course of lessons.
Strategies such as wait time and 'no hands up' are used effectively. The majority of students are actively engaged in dialogue with the teacher.	Insightful questioning and effective strategies are used consistently to check students' understanding of instructions and concepts.
The teacher's questions often focus on the learning skills being developed in lessons.	The teacher actively defines and facilitates metacognitive processes through questioning strategies, design of tasks and student interactions.
SEQUENCING CONCEPTS AND MODELLING	
Confident	**Instructor**
Lessons are well structured and planned, with each step in the students' learning clearly identified. Time is given to consolidate specific skills/concepts before the next is introduced.	The teacher is especially adept at managing the steps in each student's learning. Mini-plenaries are regularly used to consolidate the students' understanding and identify misconceptions.
The teacher regularly models approaches to tasks, noting each of the steps involved in completing them.	Worked examples are particularly well planned and modelled, with the teacher clearly identifying the principles behind each step in the process.

The teacher makes effective use of mark schemes, rubrics and concrete materials to scaffold the students' understanding of new concepts. The teacher anticipates and pre-empts likely errors or misconceptions.	The teacher's choice of scaffolds is especially well-chosen and these are adapted to suit the needs of the different students in the class. Student errors are regularly used as learning opportunities.
Lessons are clearly differentiated and challenge is evident at all ability levels. Instances of a mis-match between tasks set and a student's ability are quickly identified and rectified.	Differentiation of tasks indicates both an excellent subject knowledge and an astute judgement of the students' individual learning needs.

STAGES OF PRACTICE	
Confident	**Instructor**
The teacher allows sufficient time to introduce new concepts, asking questions to check for understanding and closely supervising students as they practise new skills.	The teacher uses a variety of strategies to enable students to assimilate new material. Students are very well prepared for independent practice and minimal independent learning time is lost through misconceptions.
Lessons are well planned with different levels of challenge to ensure that most students are secure with each step in their learning before moving on to the next.	Lessons contain a personalised level of challenge for groups of students or individual students as required, with a clear emphasis on the thorough mastery of skills and concepts.
Students are provided with ample opportunities to consolidate new skills, knowledge and concepts through class and home learning.	Lessons are well structured to ensure skills, knowledge and concepts are thoroughly understood and connections are made by students with prior learning.

LEARNING ENVIRONMENT	
Confident	**Instructor**
The learning environment is organised in such a way as to maximise teaching time. Resources are readily available to students and displays support the students' learning. Shared learning materials are of a high quality.	The arrangement of the learning environment and its resources is particularly efficient and effective. Displays are highly stimulating and support students' learning. Practical and electronic materials shared with the students are of the highest quality.

STUDENTS' RESPONSE	
Confident	**Instructor**
Students are engaged with their learning and are on task for the great majority of the lesson. They are able to work with a good degree of independence and concentration appropriate to their age. Many students demonstrate a positive mindset when approaching tasks.	Students are exceptionally focused and enthusiastic. They demonstrate positivity and resourcefulness when undertaking tasks, and will independently reflect on their learning. Students of all abilities consistently show a positive mindset.
Students are encouraged to ask questions in the course of lessons and they are able to articulate these clearly.	The students' questioning skills are very well developed and they ask thoughtful, precise questions to clarify and extend their understanding. The teacher provides frequent opportunities for students to develop and refine these skills.
RELATIONSHIPS	
Confident	**Instructor**
A good rapport between students and the teacher is evident. Interactions are warm, honest and purposeful. The teacher clearly recognises the differing needs of the students and demonstrates empathy for them. Any behavioural issues are low level and dealt with consistently by the teacher.	Relationships between students and with the teacher are exceptionally positive and mutually respectful. The students are clearly motivated by the teacher's enthusiastic and engaging manner. Low level behaviour incidents are rare.

PEDAGOGICAL RUBRIC CHECKLIST

Rosenshine's principles

- Daily review
- Present new material using small steps
- Ask questions
- Provide models
- Guide student practice
- Check for student understanding
- Obtain a high success rate
- Provide scaffolds for difficult tasks
- Independent practice
- Weekly and monthly review

Environment and Climate

- Classroom displays are stimulating, support learning, generate curiosity
- Resources are of a high quality
- Learning ethos is evident
- Routines are reinforced
- A warm and kind climate is evident
- Verbal and non-verbal communication from teacher is positive
- Boundaries are clear and followed by teacher and students
- High expectations are evident in teacher and student behaviour and work ethos

Teacher Behaviours

Explaining

- Instructions and explanations are clear
- Sufficient examples are provided
- Success is understood by all
- Previous understanding is referenced and used
- Material is re-taught as needed
- Appropriate cognitive load for all students
- Scaffolding where appropriate
- Varied instructions
- Targeted intervention
- Challenge for all students is appropriate
- Modelling is instructive
- Graphics/images are used to support conceptual understanding (dual coding)
- Material presented in small chunks, student practice after each step
- Not too much material is presented at any one time
- Teacher provides time for students to reflect on their learning
- Teacher models and articulates their own thinking

Practice and Retrieval

- 'How', 'why' and 'what happens next' are routinely used by the teacher, peers and self
- Teacher models interrogative techniques using different stems to generate different responses
- Knowledge organisers are used effectively
- Knowledge schema are used effectively
- Teacher ensures students achieve early success before attempting more complex concepts

Questioning and Feedback

- Think, pair, share
- Active boards
- A single focused question
- A series of focused questions
- Teacher asks a student to reframe a response
- Feedback from teacher is positive and encouraging
- Students raise their hands to ask a question or provide feedback
- Teacher selects students randomly to answer a question (cold calling)
- Students are comfortable to make mistakes, express uncertainty and articulate their confusion
- Students are requested to show their work to the teacher/class

Student Behaviours

- Demonstrate an understand of the classroom routine
- Demonstrate respect for teacher and peers
- Listen attentively
- Answer questions appropriately
- Ask questions of the teacher
- Ask questions of each other
- Work together collaboratively
- Work independently
- Are engaged throughout the lesson

FUTURE READY CURRICULUM
COMPETENCIES

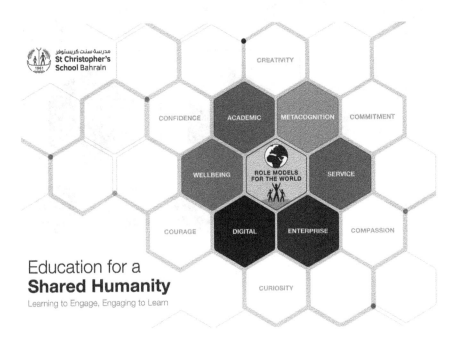

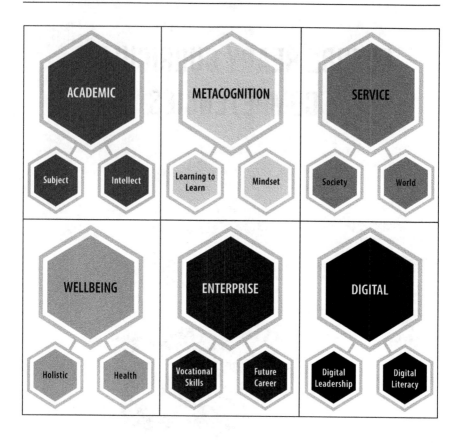

ACADEMIC COMPETENCIES

ACA01	To engage in a broad, stimulating and a well-balanced range of disciplines in order to deepen subject knowledge, skills and understanding.

This may include:

- To be able to explain why subjects being studied are important and what is expected to be learned at various stages of the learning journey.
- To develop specific cognitive models of subject knowledge, skills and understanding in order to demonstrate key learning in the pursuit of subject mastery.
- To actively engage in subject lessons by asking/answering questions and participating in class discussions, and demonstrate enthusiasm when learning.
- To continue learning outside of lessons in order to further and deepen subject knowledge, skills, and understanding.
- To develop the notion of self-identity through the interpretation of ideas, personal response and creative expression.
- To pursue extracurricular opportunities to fully explore and develop new talents, as well as build upon subject-based learning.

ACA02	To develop interdisciplinary skills and be able to apply these to subject-based learning, real-world contexts and current events.

This may include:

- To know that interdisciplinary skills enable the blending of subject boundaries to consider alternative viewpoints, make comparisons, and evaluate different concepts in order to formulate new ideas and strengthen understanding.
- To develop the interdisciplinary skills of critical thinking and analysis; research and reasoning; information handling and synthesis in order to enhance subject-based learning.
- To develop literacy abilities in the areas of speaking, listening, reading, and writing. This includes: purposeful reading, active listening, handwriting, public speaking and effective presentation delivery, in order to articulate ideas, express opinions, and engage in informed subject-related debate.

- To develop numeracy abilities to increase reasoning and application of numerical concepts. This includes using, interpreting, and presenting statistical data; applying the rules of addition, subtraction, multiplication, division, fractions, and decimals; and using graphical, spatial, and algebraic concepts to enhance subject-based learning.
- To develop deductive and inductive abilities through scientific reasoning. This involves understanding how to assess what is currently known or believed, develop testable questions, formulate hypotheses, and draw appropriate conclusions through the integration of empirical evidence and theory.
- To build cultural capital through a variety of subject-specific experiences that connect learning to real world contexts and current events.

ACA03	**To have high academic aspirations and pursue subject studies in order to fulfil educational ambitions.**

This may include:

- To be able to set S.M.A.R.T. (Specific, Measurable, Achievable, Results-oriented, and Time-bound) academic goals that are both challenging and attainable.
- To excel in a variety of subject-based assessments in both school and public examinations.
- To be able to recognise and celebrate academic successes and achievements.
- To know the pathways available for further study and how they will lead to qualifications and future education opportunities.
- To always strive to achieve your full potential and be content in knowing that you have done your best.

METACOGNITION COMPETENCIES

<table>
<tr>
<td>
MET01</td>
<td>To develop understanding of 'metacognition' and how this can be applied to enhance the conditions for learning.</td>
</tr>
</table>

This may include:

- To know that 'metacognition' is the awareness and control of your own thoughts, actions, and emotions.
- To be able to identify what successful learning looks like. This may involve the transfer between working memory and long-term memory; being able to apply knowledge and skills to new situations; and/or being able to explain a concept.
- To understand the stages of the metacognitive learning cycle and how to apply them:
  - **Planning:** Before the learning takes place, identify what needs to be learned and where to find information sources. Determine the best learning and time management strategies. Establish a learning environment that is conducive to learning.
  - **Monitoring:** During the learning process, regularly self-check any completed tasks and review progress. Know what to do if you get stuck, have a question, or if you do not understand.
  - **Evaluation:** After the learning has occurred, determine the extent to which learning objectives have been met. Recognise your own strengths and areas for improvement. In response to feedback, be proactive in correcting any errors and modifying strategies to improve future learning.

To know examples of metacognitive questions that can be used to enhance the learning process.

 METO2	**To know and be able to apply a range of high-efficacy learning strategies and study skills to improve learning.**

This may include:

- To be able to apply effective learning strategies such as:

  - **Note-taking techniques** such as the Cornell method, sketchnoting, knowledge synthesis and active reading.

  - **Partitioning** to minimise cognitive load and redundancy effect. Breaking down information or tasks into smaller, more manageable chunks.

  - **Concept mapping** to build schema, connect to prior knowledge, develop new ideas and explore new lines of inquiry.

  - **Retrieval practice** to rehearse recalling information without having it in front of you. This involves transferring information from short-term memory to long-term memory and vice versa. Strategies such as: quizzing (alternating between recalling questions and answers); flash cards (the Leitner method); creating knowledge organisers/mind maps; and using mnemonics and acronyms.

  - **Interleaving and spaced practice** to increase the depth of understanding by revisiting content on a regular basis and combining revision of different topics to strengthen knowledge.

- To be able to apply effective **study skills** such as:

  - **Time management strategies**, including: creating task lists; prioritising work; and scheduling study and leisure time.

  - **Managing distractions** to avoid the split attention effect, such as listening to lyrical music and checking messages while studying. Using methods such as the Pomodoro technique to continue working in sustained blocks of time.

  - **Personal organisation and learning environment**. Organise revision notes and learning materials (both written and digital) in folders to make them easily accessible. Establish a comfortable, quiet and tidy study space that is equipped with the materials you will need. Create a peer study network to help motivate you and/or to ask for support.

| **MET03** | **To nurture the enjoyment of learning through the cultivation of a positive mindset, curiosity, resilience and perseverance.** |

This may include:

- To understand that having a positive mindset enhances learning capacity and enables you to adapt to new experiences and overcome obstacles more easily.
- To know that positive mindset characteristics include: being optimistic with a 'can-do' attitude; the ability to visualise success; perseverance; viewing obstacles as opportunities; accepting failure as a learning opportunity; and valuing the process over the end result.
- To be able to separate criticism from feedback and accept both disappointment and success as a part of a reflective learning journey.
- To understand the impact of effort on performance and the importance of developing a strong work ethic that prioritises endeavour over perceived competence.
- To be able to take risks, especially in the presence of others, and to understand that supporting others in their learning is a powerful way to grow your self-esteem and capacity to learn.
- To enjoy learning and recognise that independent, self-directed learning creates new neural pathways and that a curious mind promotes lifelong learning.

SERVICE COMPETENCIES

| **SER01** | **To develop understanding of the concept of 'service' and how we can participate meaningfully to tackle local and global economic, social and environmental challenges.** |

This may include:

- To know that the term 'service' refers to a voluntary act of helping others, and/or taking action to support communities who face humanitarian or environmental challenges.
- To understand the distinction between service and charity. While both have value and many activities incorporate both, service emphasises active participation in the development of long-term/sustainable solutions, whereas charity typically involves the collection of goods or money for donation.

- To be able to apply the '**Think, Act, Learn**' cycle in order to identify impactful and sustainable service actions. This involves:
  - **Think:** What is the core problem to be addressed and how did it arise? Consider the short- and long-term consequences of any service intervention and whether the proposed solution is ethical and sustainable. What resources are required? What constitutes success?
  - **Act:** How can people volunteer and actively participate in order to help to solve the problem? How can passive or tokenistic behaviours be avoided? How can goals be communicated and progress tracked?
  - **Learn:** Consider the impact of the service initiative on meeting needs and/or resolving or alleviating the problem. What worked well? What could be improved? How can this be continued and/or expanded to ensure it is sustainable?
- To cultivate empathy, compassion, and concern for others through the active pursuit of a shared humanity.

SER02	**To contribute to the United Nations Sustainable Development Goals (UNSDGs) to support the global movement to build a better and more sustainable future for all.**

This may include:

- To know that the UNSDGs are a set of 17 goals aimed at ensuring that all people live in peace and prosperity by 2030. They include the following objectives:
  - **People:** to ensure healthy lives, knowledge, and in particular, the inclusion of women and children.
  - **Dignity:** to end poverty and fight inequalities.
  - **Prosperity:** to grow a strong, inclusive and transformative economy.
  - **Justice:** to promote safe and peaceful societies and strong institutions.
  - **Partnership:** to catalyse global solidarity for sustainable development.
  - **Planet:** to protect our ecosystems for all societies and our children.
- To develop awareness of how the UNSDGs goals impact the Bahrain community and in other countries around the world.
- To be able to make informed decisions about the UNSDGs in order to take action to help alleviate the challenges faced in Bahrain and internationally.

	To foster the notion of 'Global Citizenship' through increasing the awareness of rights, responsibilities, and the application of values in order to positively contribute to society while both living and working internationally.

This may include:

- To know that the term 'Global Citizen' refers to viewing our identity as one that transcends political and geographical borders, operating as a member of humanity rather than a single nationality. (Develop the notion of internationalism.)
- To develop an appreciation of global governance structures, rights and responsibilities, and the interconnectedness and interdependencies of different countries and populations.
- To recognise and appreciate differences in culture, language, religion, gender, and our common humanity, as well as develop the necessary skills for living in an increasingly diverse world. (Develop the notion of interculturalism.)
- To understand how political and geographical factors can contribute to inequality, which can result in poverty, segregation, and deprivation in different parts of the world.
- To develop the values of fairness, social justice, and inclusion to make the world a more equitable and sustainable place.

ENTERPRISE COMPETENCIES

	To develop understanding of the term 'enterprise' and how the entrepreneurial process can be applied to a variety of contexts.

This may include:

- To know that the term 'enterprise' is the willingness to take risks, demonstrate initiative, take action to innovate in order to solve a problem and/or engage in a business venture. A person who is enterprising is referred to as an 'entrepreneur'.

- To understand the various forms and purposes for enterprise:
  - **Business enterprise**, in order to make money.
  - **Ethical/social/green enterprise**, in order to benefit others or the environment.
  - **Personal enterprise**, in order to overcome one's own difficulties or accomplish a goal.
- To know that the entrepreneurial process involves the following stages:
  - **Idea generation** (identify a need or problem with possible solutions or products)
  - **Opportunity evaluation** (market analysis, risk and reward, and social, ethical, economic, and environmental impacts)
  - **Objectives and planning** (leadership and people, resources and capital, business model and milestones)
  - **Startup and launch** (product or solution launch, marketing and promotion, sales and distribution)
  - **Reflect and evaluate** (review of successes/failures, quantify profit and loss, and plan for the next phase)

ENT02	**To develop entrepreneurial skills and gain experience of applying these to a variety of educational and real-world scenarios.**

This may include:

- To be able to identify and evaluate enterprise opportunities and/or solutions to real-world problems. This may involve conducting a SWOT analysis to determine the strengths, weaknesses, opportunities, and threats associated with an idea.
- To know that the term 'idea pitch' is a presentation of an idea or concept that would persuade an audience to invest, buy, or contribute in some way to an enterprise venture.
- To be able to select, organise and present key information to effectively communicate an enterprise idea in visual form. This may involve creating a poster, presentation, graph/chart, video, advert etc.
- To be able to clearly communicate enterprise ideas and make persuasive arguments in a formal, spoken presentation and/or through a written paper. This may involve creating a digital presentation and delivering it to an audience or preparing a report for a discussion.
- To understand that many enterprise ventures rely on the formation of an effective team, which involves the concepts of leadership, collaboration and cooperation.

- To know that the term 'financial literacy', is the management of money in personal or enterprise ventures. This includes: knowing how to quantify profit and loss; consider the value of time and money while making resource decisions; taking into account ethical practices; learning about income; expenses; profit/loss accounting and forecasting; as well as investment and savings.
- To be able to create an implementation plan for an enterprise venture, detailing tasks, responsibilities, resources, costs and timescales.
- To be able to conduct market research and analyse data in order to respond to and inform future planning. This may involve constructing a questionnaire to gather feedback and analyse data.

	**To develop vocational and professional skills in order to prepare for future careers.**

This may include:

- To be able to successfully lead and motivate a team towards a common objective, while accepting accountability for the success or failure of leadership decisions and actions.
- To be able to work successfully as part of a team, demonstrating effective collaboration and communication with other team members.
- To be able to manage conflict effectively, which includes active listening, respect for opposing points of view and negotiating compromise.
- To understand that employers and further educational institutions place a high value on being able to demonstrate skills such as creativity, critical thinking, collaboration, communication and emotional intelligence.
- To understand that effective personal organisation skills consist of: time management; task prioritisation and delegation; the use of systems for organising files and resources; and stress management.
- To be able to identify and prepare for potential career paths. This may include participating in opportunities to gain experience or speaking with professionals in these fields, as well as pursuing qualifications outside of school.

DIGITAL COMPETENCIES

 DIG01	To develop understanding of the different types of digital technologies through the use of digital tools to perform increasingly complex and diverse functions.

This may include:

- To know that the term 'digital' relates to all interactions with technology (hardware, software, physical and virtual).
- To be able to identify different forms of digital technology and to select appropriate digital tools for specific tasks.
- To understand that digital technology can take many forms and that digital tools can be used for a variety of purposes.

DIG02	To increase digital literacy proficiency for research, evaluation, creation, collaboration and the communication of information.

This may include:

- To know that digital literacy is the ability to use digital technologies to research, evaluate, create, collaborate and communicate information.
- To use digital technologies proficiently in order to:
  - **Research:** use digital tools to perform effective online research.
  - **Evaluate:** use digital tools to critically evaluate and be increasingly discerning when selecting digital sources.
  - **Create:** use digital tools creatively to present information in an engaging and accessible manner that is appropriate for the target audience, and to explore solutions using digital technologies creatively to solve problems.
  - **Collaborate:** use digital tools to interact with others for an intellectual endeavour.
  - **Communicate:** use digital technologies to communicate effectively, taking into account the target audience and purpose.
- To understand how and when it is beneficial to use digital technologies to improve outcomes through the application of digital literacy functions.

To cultivate the notion of digital leadership to ensure the safe, healthy, responsible and respectful use of technologies to better our own lives and improve the circumstances of others.

This may include:

- To know that digital leadership involves the development of safe, healthy, responsible and respectful use of digital technologies.
- To know the Digital Leadership Framework of St Christopher's and acknowledge that all digital activities should endeavour to adhere to the framework.
- To be able to articulate the Digital Leadership Framework and explain its importance in ensuring online safety and cultivating Digital Leadership.
- To develop each of the key skills outlined in the Digital Leadership Framework: **Be Secure**; **Be Private**; **Be Healthy**; **Be Brave**; **Be Wise**; **Be Respectful**; **Be Kind**; **Be Inspiring**.
- To understand how to be a responsible, safe and effective user of digital technology.
- To understand the notion of digital leadership and how our own digital reputation impacts on our physical lives and opportunities.

WELLBEING COMPETENCIES

To improve our wellbeing by learning how to manage our own mental, emotional, social, and physical health.

This may include:

- To know that 'wellbeing' is our overall sense of health, happiness and life satisfaction. It is not a permanent state of happiness, but rather a state in which we can cope with the stresses and difficulties of daily life. The pursuit of positive wellbeing enables us to flourish.

- To understand that it is our responsibility to promote our own health and recognise how the following aspects of health affect our overall wellbeing: (Based on the PERMA framework.)
  - **Mental health**. This refers to a sense of fulfilment and the ability to manage daily stresses in order to perform key functions. This includes: having the capacity to learn and grow; keeping problems in perspective and being able to recover from setbacks; adapting to change and coping with uncertainty; managing stressful situations and personal anxieties. This also improves self-motivation and perseverance, both of which are necessary for success. (By working together we will support the Carnegie Award for Mental Health in Schools.)
  - **Emotional health**. This refers to our ability to control our thoughts, feelings, and behaviours. This includes: feeling good about ourselves and having an optimistic outlook; having good self-awareness and regulating positive and negative emotions. This also increases our capacity for self-reflection and resilience as a learner.
  - **Social health**. This refers to our ability to communicate with others and form positive interpersonal relationships. This includes: developing friendships; relating to and communicating with others; having a sense of belonging and connectedness; feeling secure in your own company; and being able to adapt to new social situations. This also improves our emotional intelligence and cultivates empathy for others.
  - **Physical health**. This refers to the extent that we feel physically safe and healthy. This includes eating a balanced diet, exercising on a regular basis, engaging in preventative health care, getting adequate sleep, avoiding harmful substances, and feeling secure. This also increases our energy and alertness.
- To be able to recognise potential threats to our own wellbeing and know how to access support.

WEL02	**To contribute to a culture in which people are considerate and respectful of the wellbeing of others.**

This may include:

- To understand how to positively impact and support the wellbeing needs of others. This includes: identifying changes in behaviour; being approachable and supportive; listening without passing judgement; respecting diverse perspectives; speaking considerately and in an appropriate tone; valuing the time of others and supporting them in managing priorities.
- Recognise the signs of stress and workload pressure, and be mindful of our own actions to avoid contributing to this.

- To develop the skills of empathy and emotional intelligence in order to foster a friendly, respectful and inclusive environment.
- To know that people differ in their personality traits, such as introversion and extraversion, and to take these differences into account when interacting with others.
- To understand the value of good manners and acceptable behaviour towards others.
- To develop conflict resolution skills such as: diplomacy, impartiality, de-escalation, and compassion.
- To be able to recognise when a mistake has been made and take appropriate action to rectify the situation honestly and sincerely.

WEL03	To develop compassion and mutual respect through understanding the perspectives, beliefs, and circumstances of others.

This may include:

- To understand and respect the influence of spiritual, moral, social, cultural, philosophical, and religious perspectives on individuals and society.
- To understand the existence of global inequalities and how they affect individuals and limit their access to opportunities. These include access to: health and social care; education and information; economic and political stability; human rights and justice; and food, water, shelter, and sanitation.
- To understand that each of us has a moral compass, as evidenced by the choices we make and the principles we follow. This includes acting with integrity; understanding the difference between right and wrong; respecting school policies and procedures; and observing legal and ethical boundaries.
- To know how to prevent discrimination against individuals on the basis of their race, religion, gender, age, disability, or sexual orientation.
- To uphold and demonstrate the St Christopher's core values of care, honesty, and mutual respect.

TEAM DIAGNOSTIC SHEET (THE PRINCIPALS' TRAINING CENTER)

Team attribute	Excellent	Above average	Below average	Poor
Productivity: What are the level of output and significant results of the work of this team?	4	3	2	1
Empathy: To what extent do team members listen to one another and try to understand what other members think and feel?	4	3	2	1
Roles and goals: Are the team goals clear to all members, and is each member's style or role understood and valued?	4	3	2	1
Flexibility: Does the team use different methods to make decisions, and are team members willing to consider ideas that are different from their own?	4	3	2	1
Open communication: Do team members listen to one another; can they express views that are different from those of others in the team, and resolve differences productively?	4	3	2	1
Recognition and rewards: Do team members praise contributions from one another, and feel they are mutually valued and appreciated?	4	3	2	1
Morale: Do team members feel good about being on the team; are they satisfied with the team's work?	4	3	2	1

Total score: _____

23–28   A high-performing team.

18–22   Members should continue to work in developing and using positive communication skills of listening, praising and supporting one another.

13–17   Probably experiencing a period of conflict. The team leader needs to work hard to facilitate a positive group process, provide direction and structure to accomplish goals.

7–12   The team may be in its early stages of development. Members should be as open as possible to learn more about each other. The team leader should provide direction, structure and clarify goals.

USEFUL WEBSITES

Accountability

ISC Research
  https://iscresearch.com/

Council of International Schools (CIS)
  https://www.cois.org/

New England Association of Schools and Colleges (NEASC)
  https://www.neasc.org/

International Baccalaureate Organization (IBO)
  https://www.ibo.org/

Council of British International Schools (COBIS)
  https://www.cobis.org.uk/

British Schools Overseas (BSO)
  https://www.aobso.uk/

Belonging

Race: The Power of an Illusion
  https://www.racepowerofanillusion.org/

Divserse Educators
  https://www.diverseeducators.co.uk/

Curriculum

Organisation for Economic Co-operation and Development (OECD)
  https://www.oecd.org/unitedkingdom/

United Nations Educational, Scientific and Cultural Organization (UNESCO)
  https://www.unesco.org/en

International Baccalaureate Organization (IBO)
  https://www.ibo.org/

Fieldwork Education
  https://internationalcurriculum.com/

Principals' Training Center
  https://www.theptc.org/

Networks

Association of British Schools Overseas (AOBSO)
  https://www.aobso.uk/

British Schools in the Middle East (BSME)
https://www.bsme.org.uk/

Council of British International Schools (COBIS)
https://www.cobis.org.uk/

Federation of British International Schools in Asia (FOBISIA)
https://www.fobisia.org/

The Heads' Conference (HMC) – International
https://www.hmc.org.uk/

Independent Association of Preparatory Schools (IAPS)
https://iaps.uk/

Latin American Heads Conference (LAHC)
https://www.lahc.net/

National Association of British Schools in Spain (NABSS)
https://www.nabss.org/

Online

Crown Prosecution Service (CPS)
https://www.cps.gov.uk/

Safeguarding

National Protective Security Authority (NPSA)
https://www.npsa.gov.uk/

Council of International Schools (CIS)
https://www.cois.org/

International Centre for Missing & Exploited Children (ICMEC)
https://www.icmec.org/

Trustees

The Principals' Training Center (PTC)
https://www.theptc.org/

RSAcademics
https://www.rsacademics.com/

Unity

Association for Supervision and Curriculum Developoment (ASCD)
https://www.ascd.org/

Wellbeing

International Positive Education Network (IPEN)
https://www.ipen-network.com/

Collaborative for Academic, Social, and Emotional Learning
https://casel.org/

The A–Z series focuses on the 'fun and fundamentals' of what's happening in primary, special and secondary schools today. Each title is written by a leading practitioner, adopting a series approach of reflection, advice and provocation.

As a group of authors with a strong belief in the power of education to shape and change young people's lives, we hope teachers and leaders in the UK and internationally enjoy what we have to say.

Roy Blatchford, series editor